decision that has caused us to miss our "moment," but Judy clearly conveys that although we may have missed it, God can reroute our destiny. It's not too late! You will be encouraged to live in the fullness of every God-given opportunity and be confident to run full speed ahead into your purpose as you read this relevant book. Now is YOUR time…*Don't Miss Your Moment*!

—Darlene Bishop
Copastor, Solid Rock Church
Monroe, OH

If there is anyone who can help you "maximize" your moment in this season, it is Judy Jacobs. She is a ministry gift with a relevant and passionate word for those who are reaching for their destiny with one hand, while firmly holding onto God with the other. Hear ye her!

—Dr. Teresa Hairston
Publisher, *Gospel Today* Magazine

Don't Miss Your Moment is written for every believer who is serious about living life in the power of God's anointing. Judy Jacobs lives by the principles in this book. She imparts her passion on every page. This book will help you define and recognize your moments of divine timing and seasons. Be the right person in the right place at the right time.

—Dr. Shirley Arnold
Pastor, TLC Family Church
Lakeland, FL

D0110023

Judy Jacobs reminds us of God's timing in a way that is insightful and inspirational. By helping us to understand His timing, we learn not to take for granted those moments for which He grants permission. I believe that readers will be encouraged to discard excuses, seize the day, and mount up on eagles' wings. Now, as never before, we must move quickly to redeem the time. As Judy would so aptly say, "Don't miss your moment!"

—Bishop T. D. Jakes Sr.
The Potter's House
Dallas, TX

There are great opportunities for "God moments" to happen to us every day. We don't always know how to recognize them or know what to do with them, when all the while they were right in front of us! How many "moments" have you missed that would have changed your life? Judy Jacobs is a fierce woman of God who knows how to harness a moment and bring it into manifestation. Learn from her experiences, trust her words of encouragement, and watch your life change forever!

—Martha Munizzi
Award-Winning Singer/Songwriter
International Praise and Worship Leader

Judy Jacobs is a mighty woman of God and has been given the ability to reach people not only in preaching the good news about Jesus but also in singing His praises. This book, *Don't Miss Your Moment*, will bless multitudes because it comes from the heart. I salute you, Judy.

—Dodie Osteen
Cofounder, Lakewood Church
Houston, TX

Once in a while, a book is dropped in your lap that has the power to alter the course of your life. Once in a great while, God strikes a message in the heart of His servant that is both timeless and written for such a time as this. *Don't Miss Your Moment* by Judy Jacobs is that kind of book. I believe the truths she shares will help you recognize the plan of God for your life, savor the big and little moments, understand the ways of God, and give you a longing to see His vision totally fulfilled in your life. This is the kind of book that comes along just once in a while—the kind of book that rings true.

—Pastor Joe Wingo
Founder and CEO
Angel Food Ministries

Once again Judy keeps us living on the edge of expectancy as she challenges our faith and confronts our complacency. Judy lives the words she penned on these pages, qualifying her to impart the anointing she carries into every seeker who wants to live in the fullness of their purpose.

—Karen Wheaton
Recording Artist
Founder of The Ramp
Director of Chosen

For those who are still waiting for the "big break" in life, the waiting is over. This book provides the secret keys to identifying, embracing, and experiencing the life-changing impact one defining moment can make in your life. Judy, you hit a home run with this. Great stuff!"

—Dr. Myles Munroe
BFM International
Nassau, Bahamas

Judy is a blessing in my life as well as countless others. Everything God has given her to say in this book will change lives now and forever. I love Judy!

—CeCe Winans
Award-Winning Gospel Recording Artist

So many times we miss out on God's very best because we don't know how to recognize, seize, and optimize every opportunity. In this dynamic revelation, *Don't Miss Your Moment*, Judy reveals the power of one moment and the effect it can have on your entire life. There are times when most of us feel that we have made a wrong

DON'T
MISS YOUR
MOMENT

JUDY JACOBS

Charisma
HOUSE
A STRANG COMPANY

Cover Designer: Marvin Eans
Design Director: Bill Johnson
Author Photograph © Aslan Studios, www.aslan-studios.com

Library of Congress Cataloging-in-Publication Data:
Jacobs, Judy, 1957-
   Don't miss your moment / Judy Jacobs. -- 1st ed.
      p. cm.
   Includes bibliographical references.
   ISBN 978-1-59979-233-0
   1. Christian life--Biblical teaching. I. Title.

BS680.C47J33 2008
248.4--dc22

                                   2007052285

First Edition

08 09 10 11 12 — 987654321
Printed in the United States of America

DEDICATION

THIS BOOK IS lovingly dedicated to all the mighty men and women of God in Jamie's and my life who gave us a moment in time to allow our anointing to be used on their stages. Some of them have submitted endorsements, one of them submitted a foreword, but a lot of them only Jesus can reward for helping to see us through to our moments. The Jacobs family; the Tuttle family; Danny and Debbie Murray; the Lee University family; the Emmanuel College family; the late Dr. David Horton and Lee University Campus Choir; my voice teacher and encourager, Mrs. Virginia Horton; pastors; churches; family; and friends—thank you. I love you!

To my brother Johnnie. Practically all of your life you missed moment after moment to receive Jesus as your Savior, yet in your last moment, you found Him still waiting for you to enter into eternity with Him beside you. Thank God for that "squeeze of the hand." I can't wait for the time when we will all be reunited in heaven with our Lord. What a moment that will be!

To my oldest brother, Sam. You are more like a father to all of us. Thank you for not missing your moment to make sure your younger brother made it through. You will be rewarded and will rejoice in heaven for all of eternity. Dad and Mom are so proud too!

To my fellow warriors who dared, and who still dare, to not miss their moments, to "Press, Push, and Pursue" the call of God on their lives and to make it crystal clear that their God moment will not pass them by. I say to you, go after it!

To the man of God in my life, Jamie Tuttle. Thank God that I didn't miss my one moment in life to be connected with my soul mate. I can't imagine life without you. I have cherished every moment of these past sixteen years and can't wait for the next years to come. You are the greatest decision I ever made, outside of Jesus.

To my dear, beautiful daughters, Judith Kaylee and Erica Janell. I will never ever forget that moment when I first laid eyes on each of you. What a moment that was for Dad and myself! We still look at you in awe as you continue to embrace your call and become mighty young women of God. I love you with all my heart!

To my Lord and Savior, Jesus Christ, who made me for this moment. Please help me, Father, to have a hearing ear, a seeing eye, and an open heart to never, ever, miss Your divine moments. I will love You for eternities long.

ACKNOWLEDGMENTS

N O ONE EVER accomplishes anything great without extraordinary people helping them. Such is the case with this project. With all my love and heartfelt thanks, I want to say thank you to:

Pastor Rod Parsley, for your most timely foreword. You and the World Harvest family were the very first ones to give me a stage on the "big stage." What you mean to my family and especially the body of Christ is beyond words that could ever be written. Thank God that you didn't let your moment pass by and are still going after those moments that keep you away from those you love but make big moments possible for future generations. God bless you, sir! We love and support you wholeheartedly!

Stephen and Joy Strang, who continue to believe in the Word that God has put inside me and so many others and allow us to have the humble honor and absolute privilege to share these revelations to the body of Christ. Everything you do—everything—will be rewarded.

The entire Product Development team at Strang Communications, my sincere thanks for all of your diligence in making sure that this manuscript is perfect.

A wonderful lady whom I have come to love and admire, Mrs. Kathy Deering, for all of your expertise and hard work that went into this project and goes into everything that you do. Your excellence is incomparable. May the blessings of God follow you all the days of your life.

The His Song Ministries staff, who have been there to help see this project through to completion. We appreciate and love you more than words can tell. Thank God that we are all living our moment now!

CONTENTS

CHAPTER 1

WHAT *IS* YOUR MOMENT?

I MET MY HUSBAND, Jamie, for the first time on a tour bus. I came onto the bus, tired from just having finished a concert, and saw him being interviewed by the director of the group I was part of. I wasn't feeling very chatty, and he was busy being interviewed, so I just said hello and went on about my business. Next thing I knew, he had become the drummer for the college group I was part of.

Then I started hearing some rumors that he had a crush on me. This was not good news. I thought that this guy was one of the most obnoxious people I had ever met. He was always acting silly. Now I know that he was just trying to get my attention, but it sure wasn't working the way he intended it to. My moments around him were just shy of being plain ol' nerve-racking.

Jamie wanted to date me, but I wasn't interested. He had to talk me into going out with him. Then he drove up in this banana yellow Volkswagen Beetle that I could hear coming a mile away because it had a hole in its muffler. This loud guy was not making a good impression. I would give him a chance but not much longer. Nobody on this earth could have convinced me that Jamie was the answer to my fervent prayers for a husband. How could he be?

I had been single for so long that I wasn't dating anymore at all. It's not that I didn't want to be married. I did. And I could hear my biological clock ticking. It was not only ticking; now it was starting to clang. But after much prayer and fasting, I had resolved that even if God *never* answered my prayer to have a husband to come alongside me, I would still be happy. You see, I had come from a family of twelve. That's right, *twelve kids*. I'm the baby. My momma and daddy and big brothers and big sisters just showered affection and praise on me, even after I grew up and left home. So I didn't think I needed anybody else but my family and Jesus.

And then came that first date with Jamie. That guy cut to the chase. Without any preliminaries, he said to me, "Judy, I love you, and I want to marry you." What kind of a man would say a thing like that to a woman on a first date? I thought he was a complete idiot. I didn't speak to him for the next three weeks. Eventually, we started dating again, but it took a while for me to come around. In fact, it took five long years for him to convince me that he meant it. Jamie had to be persistent, but his persistence paid off. Finally we were married.

Today I shake my head when I think how close I came to missing my moment to become the wife of this wonderful man of God, who is the most loving and caring father of our two beautiful daughters that I can imagine. Our marriage can only be described as magical. My only regret is that I wish I *had* married Jamie on the spot. That way I wouldn't have been forty years old when I had my first baby!

Missing a Big One

The New Testament church had a "moment" that should have been too important to miss. It was the Day of Pentecost, the day God bestowed His Holy Spirit on the core group of believers who had been waiting together as Jesus had told them to do. It was such an important event that we call it the birthday of the church:

And when the day of Pentecost was fully come, they were all with one accord in one place. And suddenly there came a sound from heaven as of a rushing mighty wind, and it filled all the house where they were sitting. And there appeared unto them cloven tongues like as of fire, *and it sat upon each of them.* And they were all filled with the Holy Ghost, and began to speak with other tongues, as the Spirit gave them utterance.

—Acts 2:1–4, KJV, emphasis added

The Day of Pentecost was a truly *momentous* day, a moment not to be missed. But of course many people did miss it. Rod Parsley points out:

Originally, five hundred people witnessed the Resurrection, but only one hundred twenty stayed in Jerusalem as Jesus commanded to wait on Him—doing what He said, where, when, and how He said to do it. Of these, three hundred eighty missed Pentecost because they did not obey the King. Don't miss the visitation of the Holy Spirit in your life because of disobedience.[1]

Have you ever thought about that before? What happened to all those people who missed their moment of visitation? They missed Pentecost! Three hundred eighty of them. They must have drifted off, having decided that something, somewhere, was more important than Jesus's specific command to stay in the city until they were clothed with power from on high. Jesus had come back from the dead and had showed Himself to them many times, and then He told them clearly what they were supposed to do next:

And being assembled together with them, He *commanded them* not to depart from Jerusalem, but to wait for the Promise of the Father, "which," He said, "you have heard from Me; for

John truly baptized with water, but you shall be baptized with the Holy Spirit not many days from now."...[and] you shall receive power when the Holy Spirit has come upon you; and you shall be witnesses to Me in Jerusalem, and in all Judea and Samaria, and to the end of the earth."

—Acts 1:4–5, 8, emphasis added

Granted, none of them were sure what that meant. What exactly would they be waiting for? Some kind of divine empowerment? What did that mean? More than half of the believers ended up deciding that they didn't want to wait that long. They probably figured, "I've got a family to take care of, business to transact, things to do..." They didn't want to put their daily lives on hold for an indefinite period of time. Those men and women gave up on waiting. As a result, they missed their divine moment on the Day of Pentecost. They missed the cloven tongues of fire. They missed the gift of tongues. They missed receiving the baptism of the Holy Spirit.

> THE BIGGEST AND MOST IMPORTANT MOMENT OF ALL IS THE MOMENT WHEN YOU GAVE YOUR LIFE OVER TO THE LORDSHIP OF JESUS CHRIST.

Now, I hope that a number of those folks who missed all that happened caught up with the disciples later and did receive the Holy Spirit. Many of them may have heard the news along with the thousands of people who came to find out what all the fuss was about. Although they may have missed the big moment, they got in on the results. But I am sure many of them just went home, some even to faraway cities, and they never heard about the Holy Spirit at all. They really and truly missed their moment.

That's something to think about.

WHAT ARE YOU WAITING FOR?

What do I mean when I say don't miss your moment? What should you be looking for? What should you be waiting for? Am I talking only about those one-time, big, important, life-changing moments like finding the person you're going to marry or receiving the Holy Spirit? Or am I talking about smaller moments too? What *is* a moment?

How should you wait for your moment? What should you be doing in the meantime? And, God forbid, what if you—like all those people on the Day of Pentecost—make the wrong decision and you miss your moment? Can you have a second chance or not? These are good questions, and as you read this book, you will discover the answers.

BIG AND NOT-SO-BIG MOMENTS

The biggest and most important moment of all is the moment when you gave your life over to the lordship of Jesus Christ. But that's not the only time God is going to touch your life. He's interested in your whole life, and He has plans for you. He wants to conform you to His image, and He has plotted out the details of your life. He wants you to fulfill your destiny. Therefore, your life ends up being made up of moments both large and small, those special times when God touches you and a shift takes place.

A moment is when a divine spark "catches" in your life—it catches on fire and starts to burn. It has been said that the anointing is caught instead of taught. I believe that a moment happens when you catch it straight from God, as a catcher in baseball would catch a pitch from a pitcher. You just have to position yourself to catch it.

A moment is when something changes in God's favor. It may be foundational and all important, like deciding to make Jesus your Lord and Savior or accepting the Holy Spirit or deciding who is going to be your husband or wife. Or it may be seasonal and somewhat less significant, like deciding where to live or even which book to read. Sometimes a moment will kind of sneak up on you and grab you. More often than not, you will have to sneak up on it and grab *it* yourself.

> YOUR WHOLE LIFE IS GOING TO BE A SERIES OF GOD MOMENTS THAT BUILD ON EACH OTHER. YOU BELONG TO HIM, SO EXPECT IT.

At the time, you often can't grasp the importance of it. You just have to show up at the right time and do the right thing. Your assignment is to walk in obedience to the One who is the Lord of all of your moments. The ramifications will show up later.

Your God moments are when you see in operation—in yourself—the same power that dwelled in Jesus Christ of Nazareth when He walked on this earth. The Bible tells us, "Jesus of Nazareth was anointed by God with the Holy Spirit and with power, and he went around doing good" (Acts 10:38, TLB). You know what? *The same power that raised Jesus from the dead is in you. The same power that got Him up is going to get you up.* Every believer needs to understand this. It's part of the good news.

God's power is quickening your mortal body. God handpicked you to be one of His representatives on Earth, just as He handpicked Jesus to be born as a man and to be anointed with the Holy Spirit and with power. Before the foundation of the world, Jesus was the lamb who was slain. Before you were conceived in your mother's womb, even five, six, seven, ten generations before that, God had you on His mind. He picked you out. He knew He would give you His Holy Spirit.

I want you to really *get* this: the same Spirit who was in Jesus is in you. He dwells in anybody who has accepted Him as Lord and Savior. He has kindled a fire in your heart, and sometimes He comes and blows on it so that it blazes brighter and shows you how to walk into some dark place. Even before Jesus came as a man, people who believed in God met Him. Sometimes they missed their moment to meet God, but other times, they turned to meet Him. God has always consistently reached into the lives of people and has made it possible for them to do great exploits. The same God who was with Moses was with Joshua. The same God who was with Elijah was with Elisha. When your moment comes, you can step into it with as much confidence as they did.

Your whole life is going to be a series of God moments that build on each other. You belong to Him, so expect it. Don't get distracted and miss any of them. Even if you have to wait a long time for a particular moment to arrive, keep waiting with expectant faith, ready to step into it.

We get in such a hurry for God to reveal things. Often the Lord tells us to wait. Sometimes waiting is the hardest thing we have to do—keeping ourselves filled with faith as we wait for God's promise to be fulfilled, keeping a positive outlook, anticipating the arrival of a long-awaited answer to a prayer, telling ourselves, "I will not be weary in well doing, knowing that I will reap in due season if I do not faint."[2]

Moments in the Bible

There are God moments all over the place in the Bible. We are familiar with the stories, but we may have not noticed the moments in them. Here's one that happened shortly after the Day of Pentecost:

> Peter and John went to the Temple one afternoon to take part in the three o'clock prayer service. As they approached the Temple, a man lame from birth was being carried in. Each day he was put beside the Temple gate, the one called the Beautiful Gate, so he could beg from the people going into the Temple. When he saw Peter and John about to enter, he asked them for some money.
>
> Peter and John looked at him intently, and Peter said, "Look at us!" The lame man looked at them eagerly, expecting some money. But Peter said, "I don't have any silver or gold for you. But I'll give you what I have. In the name of Jesus Christ the Nazarene, get up and walk!"
>
> Then Peter took the lame man by the right hand and helped him up. And as he did, the man's feet and ankles were instantly healed and strengthened. He jumped up, stood on his feet, and began to walk! Then, walking, leaping, and praising God, he went into the Temple with them.
>
> All the people saw him walking and heard him praising God. When they realized he was the lame beggar they had seen so often at the Beautiful Gate, they were absolutely astounded!
>
> —Acts 3:1–10, NLT

The lame man did not miss his moment. Do you see how important it is to *do something* when your moment appears? The lame man had to look at Peter and John when they told him to, and he had to cooperate when they pulled him to his feet. He had to be willing to let Peter and John be involved, but he couldn't rely on their human strength alone. They couldn't heal him, but God could—and He did. What a moment!

In a way, it was also a moment for Peter and John because it was such an important miracle in the life of the new church. They could have brushed the man aside and just kept going. After all, they had been on their way to the afternoon service. They probably did miss their scheduled time of prayer because of what occurred. But they recognized God's move. God was at the Beautiful Gate that day. Whatever was scheduled in the temple didn't matter. Peter and John wouldn't have missed that moment for all the prayer meetings in the world.

Now Is the Time

The Bible is filled with words like "the time has come," "immediately," and "now is the time." In the following examples, I have put the key words in italics:

> *Now is the time!* For the LORD has said, "I have chosen David to save my people Israel from the hands of the Philistines and from all their other enemies."
>
> —2 Samuel 3:18, NLT

> Jesus said to him, "Go your way; your faith has made you well." And *immediately* he received his sight and followed Jesus on the road.
>
> —Mark 10:52

As soon as Judas left the room, Jesus said, "*The time has come for the Son of Man to enter into his glory, and God will be glorified because of him.*"

—John 13:31, NLT

God's timing is what they were looking for—God's moment for right then—and we are looking for His timing too. Not yesterday's time or next year's time. Today, now, this moment. What is God saying? What is He doing? How quickly can a person say yes?

MOSES'S MOMENTS

Not all of God's moments are instantaneous. The lame man walked instantly, but sometimes a moment jump-starts a process, and the process takes quite a while to work itself out, with important moments all along the way. Moses gave us a good example of that.

Let's start with the burning bush. How could he miss that moment? Not only did it burn without being consumed, but it also *talked*. Moses took off his shoes on such holy ground, and he listened well. (See Exodus 3.) It took him a little while to agree to the assignment, but he didn't miss his moment to speak to Pharaoh. No, sir. He marched right up into the palace where he used to live, and he demanded, "Let my people go!" (See Exodus 4–12.)

Pharaoh wasn't too cooperative. God had to force his hand a little. Then after that last and worst plague, he relented: "Pharaoh sent for Moses and Aaron during the night. 'Get out!' he ordered. 'Leave my people—and take the rest of the Israelites with you! Go and worship the LORD as you have requested. Take your flocks and herds, as you said, and be gone'" (Exod. 12:31–32, NLT).

It was the moment for the children of Israel to be liberated. We know the story well. They left, but their way was blocked by the

Red Sea, and the Egyptian army was hot on their heels. Moses didn't miss his next moment either, even though the situation seemed to be impossible. He obeyed when God told him to raise his staff over the water to part it, he obeyed as he told the people what to do, and he obeyed when he raised his staff again so that the walls of water came crashing down on the Egyptians. (See Exodus 14:15–31.)

> OUR OBEDIENCE CONNECTS US WITH GOD'S GRACE AND POWER, AND WE GAIN ANOTHER PART OF THE DESTINY HE HAS SET BEFORE US.

Now they were wandering in the desert, guided by the pillar of cloud and fire. After a while, Moses sent spies into the land that God had told them they would possess. What a moment! Soon they would occupy a land of milk and honey. Most of the men who went to spy out the land reported to Moses, "We entered the land you sent us to explore, and it is indeed a bountiful country—a land flowing with milk and honey. Here is the kind of fruit it produces. But the people living there are powerful, and their towns are large and fortified. We even saw giants there, the descendants of Anak!" (Num. 13:27–28, NLT).

Caleb was one of the spies, and he had a different report: "Caleb tried to quiet the people as they stood before Moses. 'Let's go at once to take the land,' he said. 'We can certainly conquer it!'" (Num. 13:30, NLT). Caleb was ready to seize the moment, and so was Joshua:

> They [Caleb and Joshua] said to all the people of Israel, "The land we traveled through and explored is a wonderful land! And if the

LORD is pleased with us, he will bring us safely into that land and give it to us. It is a rich land flowing with milk and honey. Do not rebel against the LORD, and don't be afraid of the people of the land. They are only helpless prey to us! They have no protection, but the LORD is with us! Don't be afraid of them!"

—Numbers 14:7–9, NLT

But the other men who had explored the land with him disagreed. "We can't go up against them! They are stronger than we are!" So they spread this bad report about the land among the Israelites: "The land we traveled through and explored will devour anyone who goes to live there. All the people we saw were huge. We even saw giants there, the descendants of Anak. Next to them we felt like grasshoppers, and that's what they thought, too!"

—Numbers 13:31–33, NLT

Which ones did the people listen to? The fearful spies. And they put so much pressure on Moses that he made the wrong decision. On that occasion, Moses and the people of Israel missed their moment, big-time. That decision had huge ramifications.

You see, all God moments involve choices. Moses and the others had to choose to obey God—or not. So do we. Our obedience connects us with God's grace and power. We choose to move in and take territory. As a result, we gain another part of the destiny He has set out before us. But if we choose to listen to our fears and our hesitations, it's as if we are listening to those spies who gave that bad report.

It's deadly serious business to make the wrong choice and miss your moment. It can be costly. It cost the Israelites forty more years in the wilderness, with thousands of deaths along the way. Remember, these are the same people who had witnessed more miraculous events in a row than the world had ever seen before—and still they missed their moment. Not only that, but look what it cost Moses—he didn't get to enter either.

Now, God did give them another chance, but it wasn't even the same group of people, except for Caleb and Joshua. It was the children and grandchildren of the tribes of Israel who got to try again, and that time they made it. (The story is told in the Book of Joshua.) Yes, sometimes God lets us have a second chance. But how much better would it be if we would only obey the first time? Forty years is a long time, a generation.

Making "Momentous" Choices

So, is this some kind of new gospel message? No, not at all. It's just a different way of looking at the way God works in our lives. I want you to recognize that God has His hand on your life and that He has a plan and a purpose for you. I want you to get so fired up in your faith that you will never miss your moment. God wants to connect with you. He doesn't want to stay far away from you. Contrary to what the devil would have you believe, He wants to bless you, and He wants to use you for the sake of other people. He wants to remind you of how His kingdom works.

Be patient, but don't wait too long.

In order not to miss your God moments, you need to get your timing right. You need to be patient, and at the same time you need to be ready to jump. Don't worry; that's not as hard to do as it sounds.

King Saul is a good example of somebody who wasn't patient enough to wait for his moment. The prophet Samuel gave him the clear command of the Lord, but he did not obey it:

Samuel also said to Saul, "The Lord sent me to anoint you king over His people, over Israel. Now therefore, heed the voice of the words of the Lord. Thus says the Lord of hosts: 'I will punish Amalek for what he did to Israel, how he ambushed him on the way when he came up from Egypt. Now go and attack Amalek, and utterly destroy all that they have, and do not spare them. But kill both man and woman, infant and nursing child, ox and sheep, camel and donkey.'"

—1 Samuel 15:1–3

And Saul attacked the Amalekites, from Havilah all the way to Shur, which is east of Egypt. He also took Agag king of the Amalekites alive, and utterly destroyed all the people with the edge of the sword. But Saul and the people spared Agag and the best of the sheep, the oxen, the fatlings, the lambs, and all that was good, and were unwilling to utterly destroy them.

—1 Samuel 15:7–9

As a result, the Lord revealed the hard truth to Samuel: He now was going to reject Saul as the king of Israel because he had missed his moment. Saul had disobeyed God's command. That meant that Samuel had the unpleasant task of telling Saul that he was going to have to suffer God's rejection. Samuel told him:

Why then did you not obey the voice of the Lord?...
Has the Lord as great delight in burnt offerings and
    sacrifices,
As in obeying the voice of the Lord?
Behold, to obey is better than sacrifice,
And to heed than the fat of rams.
For rebellion is as the sin of witchcraft,
And stubbornness is as iniquity and idolatry.

> Because you have rejected the word of the LORD,
> He also has rejected you from being king.
> > —1 Samuel 15:19, 22–23

What a difference *obedience* would have made!

The other Saul, the one who became Paul in the New Testament church, gives us an example of being *quick* to obey God. It seems that Paul never missed his God moments. Even from the beginning, he obeyed so quickly that the other disciples had a hard time keeping up with him. They didn't know whether or not they could trust his conversion experience because it was so sudden. Less than a week elapsed between his Damascus Road conversion and the beginning of his preaching ministry.

> *Immediately* he preached the Christ in the synagogues, that He is the Son of God. Then all who heard were amazed, and said, "Is this not he who destroyed those who called on this name in Jerusalem, and has come here for that purpose, so that he might bring them bound to the chief priests?" But Saul increased all the more in strength, and confounded the Jews who dwelt in Damascus, proving that this Jesus is the Christ.
> > —Acts 9:20–22, emphasis added

Paul didn't wait to see how everybody was going to respond. He didn't take a poll or a survey first. He just plunged in with both feet, preaching the faith as passionately as he had been persecuting it formerly. He stepped out of the old season of his life and into the new one, not only without missing his moment but also without missing even a single step.

That's the way God wants us to do it too. He has a magnificent design for each of our lives, and He wants us to step into it. His voice is not muffled. He makes sure it's clear because He wants us to understand.

The reason I said you don't have to worry about getting the timing right is because it is always simply a matter of obedience. Did you just hear Him say something? Then obey it. You say you don't know how He wants you to obey? Just ask Him. He'll make that clear too.

Oswald Chambers said, "God not only expects me to do His will, but He is in me to do it."[3]

Know the times and seasons.

God is the Lord of your times and seasons, so He's the Lord of changing them. Daniel proclaimed:

> Blessed be the name of God forever and ever,
> For wisdom and might are His.
> And *He changes the times and the seasons*;
> He removes kings and raises up kings;
> He gives wisdom to the wise
> And knowledge to those who have understanding.
> He reveals deep and secret things;
> He knows what is in the darkness,
> And light dwells with Him.
> —Daniel 2:20–22, emphasis added

God is the only one who can change your times and seasons, and He is the only one who can explain to you what He's doing. God knows your tomorrows like you know your yesterdays. He can reveal or conceal whatever He wants to. For the most part, He wants to reveal things to you, even "deep and secret things," things nobody else knows, not even the wise.

He is the giver of *wisdom*. He wants to give it to you. He wants to give you *knowledge and understanding* too. Did you know that there are some things that you know that you don't know? He is in you to reveal the deep and the secret things through His Holy Spirit. He is over everything, and He wants to make you aware of what you need to know. He does not want to keep you in the dark.

If He wants to open up the Red Sea, He can. (And He will tell a Moses that it's time to march the people through the middle.) If He wants to get water out of a rock, He can. If He wants to raise His friend Lazarus from the dead, He can. And if He wants to change your situation, He can and He will. What the enemy has meant for bad in your life, God means for good. Expect your times and seasons to change, and expect Him to help you keep on track so you won't miss what He is doing.

God will give you *favor.* David wrote, "But You, O LORD, shall endure forever.... You will arise and have mercy on [us], for the time to favor...yes, the set time, has come" (Ps. 102:12–13). What David accomplished in his life had nothing to do with where he started out and everything to do with the fact that God had picked him out. God changed David's times and seasons over and over, always for the better, and He will do the same for you.

Before they left Egypt, the people of Israel did as Moses told them, and God gave them favor because of it:

> And the people of Israel did as Moses had instructed; they asked the Egyptians for clothing and articles of silver and gold. The LORD caused the Egyptians to look favorably on the Israelites, and they gave the Israelites whatever they asked for. So they stripped the Egyptians of their wealth!
> —Exodus 12:35–36, NLT

If you are obedient to God, not only is He going to give you favor, but He is also going to give you *release*. Besides that, God is going to give you *increase*. Here's how He expressed it to Abraham:

> By Myself I have sworn, says the LORD, because you have done this thing, and have not withheld you son, your only son— blessing I will bless you, and in multiplying I will multiply your descendants as the stars of the heaven and as the sand which is on the seashore; and your descendants shall possess the gate of their enemies. In your seed all the nation of the earth shall be blessed, because you have obeyed My voice.
>
> —Genesis 22:16–18

God wants to set you free from your enemies, favor you with blessings, and make you fruitful. He wants to turn around your family situation. He wants to release everything that is bound up and bind everything up that is keeping you from Him. (See Matthew 16:19; 18:18.)

God always outdoes Himself. When He changes our times and seasons, His abundance overflows every time. He measures it out according to our responsiveness. Jesus said to give, and you will receive. Your gift will return to you in full—pressed down, shaken together to make room for more, running over, and poured into your lap. The amount you give will determine the amount you get back (Luke 6:38).

Your Father in heaven delights in blessing you. He delights to shift and change your times and seasons to make everything conform to His plan. He's ready to make changes on your behalf. Are you ready to say yes to Him?

Move from ordinary to extraordinary.

Did you know that it doesn't matter where you start? It matters where you finish. To get to the finish line, you need to run the race with excellence, empowered by His grace.

We love and serve a God who is perfect in every way. He wants to bring us into His perfection, and He wants us to want what He wants. He wants everything in you to line up with His perfect order and peace and love and strength.

God calls people who are willing to push hard. He knows that if you can take it, you can make it. He gives more grace to you as you proceed. He takes you from the ordinary to the *extraordinary.* The difference between extraordinary and ordinary is five letters: E-X-T-R-A.

> GOD'S SPIRIT
> INSIDE YOU IS LIKE
> YOUR INTERNAL
> NAVIGATION SYSTEM,
> AND YOU NEED TO
> PAY ATTENTION TO IT.

E stands for *equipped.* To rise up to a level of excellence, you need to be equipped with the armor of the Spirit (Eph. 6:10–18)—the belt of truth, the breastplate of righteousness, the shoes of the gospel of peace, the shield of faith, the helmet of salvation, and the sword of the Spirit. You need to keep them on all the time. You need to sleep with them and eat with them on. You need to be so familiar with them that you use them instinctively. If you're not equipped for battle, you're still ordinary, and you are bait for Satan's attacks.

X stands for *excitement.* Excitement is contagious. You can catch it from someone else, and other people can catch it from you. I don't know about you, but I want to be around people who are excited about their God and what God is doing in the earth. The Bible says that iron sharpens iron. I want to always be around people who intimidate me to greatness—someone who is more excited than I am, who has more faith than I do, who knows the Word better than I do. My husband and I love to play golf together. What really excites both of us is playing with someone who is better than we are so we can learn. This leads me to my next letter...

T stands for *teaching* and *training*. The more teaching and training you receive, the more you can turn around and give to others.

R stands for *righteousness*. Extraordinary excellence demands a righteous walk. "Purify yourselves, you who carry the vessels of the LORD" (Isa. 52:11, NASU). You don't want to do anything that would compromise your walk with a God of perfect love.

A stands for *action*. Yes! All the equipping and teaching and excitement and righteousness in the world don't count for much if there's no action. Faith without works is dead (James 2:20). You have to *do* something with all of those blessings.

E-X-T-R-A: Extra determination, extra commitment, extra faith, extra everything. It makes you able to be extraordinary in every way. If you are extraordinary, you pursue excellence, which comes from painstaking conscientiousness. Excellence is hard work, but it is so worthwhile. You want more of God? You want to reflect Him to the people around you? Then you will reach for excellence in everything you do, asking for His perfect grace every step of the way.

And by the way, are you the "least" in some way? Are you the youngest, the least experienced, the least gifted, or the least something else? Because if you are, that will be your best launching pad for a life of excellence. God chooses the least (Luke 9:48). Gideon was the weakest man of a little tribe. David was the youngest and least significant of his brothers. Paul was the least of the apostles, but he said, "When I am weak, then I am strong" (2 Cor. 12:10).

The God who is inside you is greater than the whole world put together. One little word breathed from Him destroys the darkness and turns on all the lights.

Follow your internal navigation system.

The God who is inside you will surely tell you whether to turn to the right or to the left, whether to stop or to start. His Spirit inside you is like your internal navigation system, and you need to pay attention to it.

It's a little bit like those talking navigational systems that some cars have. You know, you start driving and they start talking: "Take the second right on Main Street. Turn left at the intersection of Main Street and Second Street. You have reached your destination." If you turn off the system, you won't know where to go. You might not even know when you get there. If you disobey the clear instructions of the voice and turn left instead of right, you won't get there, either.

Of course, God's voice is not usually broadcasting loudly inside you. His voice is quiet, and you need to have a quiet mind and spirit in order to hear it. You have to listen intently. You have to determine whether what you're hearing is His voice or some other voice. Is it consistent with His character? Can you feel your faith rising up to meet it?

Many times, people miss their moments because they aren't even underway. It's like the car is still in the garage. Your car can be well equipped with the latest navigational device, but it won't do you a bit of good if you don't put the key into the ignition and *go* someplace. If you don't take action, nothing will happen. If you fail to plan, you plan to fail.

Learn to use your authority.

Don't wait to see how everybody else responds before you say, "I'll get involved." If you do that, you may wait too long, and you may miss your moment. You need to recognize the Father's authority in your life as well as the voice of His direction. You need to recognize your own authority, which comes from Him.

Your voice represents your authority, just as God's voice represents His authority. He speaks, and things come into being. He speaks, and the darkness flees. When you open your mouth and speak, the darkness flees too. Even the darkness inside you will flee if you will talk to yourself. I do it all the time.

> DON'T TRY TO CONVINCE GOD THAT HE HAS CALLED THE WRONG PERSON TO THE WRONG THING. INSTEAD, STEP OUT AND EXPECT TO SEE HIM MOVE THE MOUNTAINS THAT MAY BE IN YOUR WAY.

The Bible says, "Submit to God. Resist the devil and he will flee from you" (James 4:7). Paul said, "I follow after, if that I may apprehend that for which also I am apprehended of Christ Jesus" (Phil. 3:12, KJV). You have to go after your flesh and resist the devil and apprehend the calling that God has installed inside you.

What is your calling? You have to know what it is. You have to understand what your anointing is all about. You have to know who you are in Christ, and you have to tell your flesh and the devil who you are in Christ. Let me remind you, the devil has power, but his power is very, very limited because what the devil does not have is *authority*. You have more authority in your pinky that the devil has in the world.

The Bible says that John the Baptist was the "greatest among men," but also that "the least in the kingdom of God is greater than he" (Matt. 11:11; Luke 7:28). That means that my little daughter is greater than John the Baptist. The same power that raised Jesus Christ from the dead is in my little daughter—and inside you. Our children don't get a junior Holy Spirit, and neither do we receive less of the Holy Spirit than Jesus Christ Himself did. That same power resides in you, and it can resurrect everything that is dead in you. It can wake up everything that has been asleep. You can rise up in more power and authority than you knew you possessed, and you can operate on a whole new level of it. The devil will have to tuck his tail down between his legs and run.

If you pursue everything God wants you to have, you will assume your position in the kingdom realm, and you will see God manifest Himself the way He wants to. You will breathe and move and speak with His authority. "Greater is He who is in you than he who is in the world."

The One in you is greater! The One in you is mightier! The God of glory will shine out through you with power. Get ready!

Step out!

I love my friend Joyce Meyer. A few years ago I was sitting with her before it was time for her to speak that night, and I didn't really want to bother her. You know, she *is* Joyce Meyer. But she said, "Come here and tell me what's going on in your life."

At the time, Jamie and I were trying to make some major decisions, so I started telling her about that. And she had some advice for me that I'm sure she's given to other people. She said to me, "Judy, sometimes you've just got to step out and find out. If you never step out, you'll never know, and you'll always think, 'I wonder what would have happened if I would have stepped out.'"

I love to hear her tell the story of when the Lord called her to preach. At first, her response was hesitant. She said, "You know, Lord, I am a woman. People don't like woman preachers." Then she said, "I could almost hear the Lord say, 'You know, Joyce, you are exactly right. I forgot all about that. I don't know how I made that mistake. Listen, don't even worry about what I just said. I made a mistake. I can't call women to preach. That's right. Yeah.'"

The point she was making was that God always knows what He is doing. If He tells you to start doing something, just step out and do it. Don't try to convince Him that He has called the wrong person to the wrong thing. Instead, step out and expect to see Him move the mountains that may be in your way.

Keep things in perspective. You don't have to get flaky or weird to obey what He tells you. What He tells you will make sense to you, and you will understand that the times and the seasons are changing. God opens doors, and He also shuts them. Determine whether you have an open door in front of you. If you do, step through it, fully convinced that He who is in you is greater than he who is in the world. Don't miss your moment!

> For the grace of God has been revealed, bringing salvation to all people. And we are instructed to turn from godless living and sinful pleasures. We should live in this evil world with wisdom, righteousness, and devotion to God, while we look

forward with hope to that wonderful day when the glory of our great God and Savior, Jesus Christ, will be revealed.

He gave his life to free us from every kind of sin, to cleanse us, and to make us his very own people, totally committed to doing good deeds.

—Titus 2:11–14, NLT

CHAPTER 2

PURSUING YOUR MOMENT

O NCE IN A while, you will stumble right into your moment. It's like when you bump into an old friend on the street when you least expect to. What a wonderful surprise! You throw your arms around each other and exclaim, "Wow! Hi! Good to see you!"

But of course this doesn't happen very often. Most of the time, your old friends don't bump into you, and your moments won't bump into you either. You need to go looking for them. You need to make some kind of an effort. The whole kingdom of God is like that. Here's what Jesus said:

> Ask, and it will be given to you; seek, and you will find; knock, and it will be opened to you. For everyone who asks receives, and he who seeks finds, and to him who knocks it will be opened.... If you then, being evil, know how to give good gifts to your children, how much more will your Father who is in heaven give good things to those who ask Him!
> —Matthew 7:7–8, 11

I don't have any trouble agreeing with that scriptural kingdom principle; do you? But come to think about it, how, exactly, do you go about this? What's actually involved in the process of seeking to bump into my next God moment? Am I already doing it or not? How do you know?

Mom Showed Me

My mom was seeking God all the time, and she showed me what it looks like. (With twelve kids, she *had* to. But I think she would have done it even if she had never had kids.) Her main passion was a passion for God, and she sought Him with all of her heart.

She'd get up real early in the morning to seek Him. I'd hear her. She would rise up out of her bed as early as three o'clock in the morning, and she'd try to find a secluded place to talk to God. You have to understand, she did not pray silently. As a matter of fact, she prayed loudly, even if she got so loud that she woke some of us up. She did this all the time. I don't think she ever missed a chance to pray.

> Understand that there's no quick microwave version of how to "cook up" your moment. Just keep looking for it even when it seems to be far out of reach.

Sunday church was never enough for her. She took it upon herself to have prayer meetings at our house. People would come from all over the community, and they would stay for hours. They knew that they would encounter God at Sister Jacobs's house. This wasn't just a nice ladies' night out with conversation and food and drink and a little twenty-minute prayer time thrown in. Those people came to *pray*, and that's all they did.

28

I grew up with this going on, week in and week out. My older sisters would pray too, even in the afternoon between school and their chores. Apart from school and work, all we knew was church. It made me the way I am today—passionate and bold toward the enemy, secure in my standing with God, not timid about asking Him for just about anything.

What I saw my mom doing was *pursuing* God. She was relentless. She was tireless. She ate, slept, and breathed a life of passionate pursuit. And you know what? She got results. As far as I could see, she never missed her moment.

THE ART OF THE PURSUIT

Pursuit is a very active word. When you're pursuing something, you're moving after it. You're not passive. Even if you're sitting still for a period of time, you stay alert, actively watching and expecting something to happen.

Your moment might appear suddenly, or it might take years. When you're pursuing God's moments, you won't get discouraged if it turns into a long haul. You understand that there's no quick microwave version of how to "cook up" your moment. You just have to keep looking for it even when it seems to be far out of reach.

My mom didn't become a spiritual powerhouse instantly on the first night she got up to pray. She didn't get all of her prayers answered on day one. She kept pursuing God until He answered her current request. And then she applied her energy to pursue God some more.

For everybody, this is a process. The particular moment you're interested in might be just around the next corner, but it also might not be. Your moment might be forty years down the road. If God sent it today, you might not have everything in place for it yet. You *will* have everything in place when the time is right. Even if it seems that you have missed your moment, trust that God will reposition you next time around and that He is always faithful to complete what He starts in you. So you just keep at it. Keep waiting and praying and watching.

You are positioning yourself to *be* there when your moment arrives. You are positioning yourself both inside (in your heart and soul and spirit) and outside (circumstantially and relationally).

At this point, you may be wondering, "Exactly *how* can I position myself so that I don't miss my moment? I want some practical ideas." That's what I want to give you in the rest of this chapter.

THE ART OF WAITING

Waiting rooms are not my favorite places. I get impatient. I sit there and jiggle my feet. I sigh. I have so many other things to do. Besides, those magazines are so *old*.

Waiting for God to show up can be a lot harder than waiting for a doctor's appointment. Even on the doctor's slowest day, I know I will get out of that waiting room after a few hours. Waiting for God is a little different. Waiting for God can take an entire lifetime, and the magazines are optional. You can make a whole career of waiting for God.

So, although it seems contradictory to say so, *waiting* is part of *pursuing* God's moments in your life. Waiting—and being willing to wait—is a very important and practical part of any divine appointment.

It's not a passive thing at all. Oh, no. When you are waiting, you are quite active. On the negative side, you are busy fending off all of your impatient fretfulness. On the positive side, you are busy growing in your faith and trust. You are getting rid of distractions and refining your focus on Jesus. You are listening—waiting for your name to be called.

The Bible says, "Be still and know that I am God" (Ps. 46:10). If you want to know God better, then you have to get still, get quiet. When you have hushed your soul and spirit and body, you will start to put down roots and draw up strength.

The Bible also says, "In quietness and confidence shall be your strength" (Isa. 30:15). You have to get to a special place, alone with God. If you are really serious about laying hold of your destiny, you have to realize that it will be a process, one handhold at a time, and a lot of it will happen when you're closeted with God, waiting, pondering, soaking up His presence. It's part introspection, part prayer, part sitting at His feet where you learn and grow and get transformed so that you reflect His image.

It is not something you can achieve in your own strength. You know already what will

> WAITING IS AN ACKNOWLEDGEMENT OF GOD'S TIMES AND SEASONS.

happen if you think your own strength is sufficient. (You will fall flat on your nose—in public probably.) God wants to provide for you, but to do that He needs you to be aware of your insufficiency. You *need* Him. Waiting is an expression of your desire for more of Him.

I have found encouragement in Rod Parsley's words:

> One of the best things that can happen to you is to face an obstacle that is impossible to overcome by yourself. Then, when you are victorious, everyone must say, "It was God."
>
> ...The future is unlimited in God. You don't have to feel bound by the things that once bound you. You have Someone inside you who is greater than anything you will ever face.[1]

God is stronger than any obstacle or any human being, and He wants to have an opportunity to show you how strong He is. That can't happen if you're noisily charging around full-steam ahead, acting like you have everything you need already. Sure, once in a while He will knock you off your high horse as He did with Paul on the road to Damascus, but normally, that's just not the way God works.

The humble English preacher Smith Wigglesworth (who was known for saying, "Only believe!") explained how God works with us:

> Sometimes we are tested on the lines of faith. For twenty-five years Abraham believed God. God said to him: "Thy wife shall have a son." Every year his wife grew weaker. He saw the wrinkles and her puny, weak condition. Did he look at it? No—he looked at the promise. For twenty-five years God tested him; but he gave glory to God, and considered neither Sarah's body nor his own. And as he did so, God said, "Yes, Abraham."
>
> Listen to what the Word says: "Now it was not written for his sake alone...but for us also...if we believe on him that raised up Jesus our Lord from the dead; who was delivered for our offences, and was raised again for our justification" (Rom. 4:23–25).
>
> All who believe are blessed along with faithful Abraham. God wants to show us that nothing is impossible to those who believe.[2]

Waiting is also an acknowledgement of God's times and seasons. Very often, we wait simply because it's not time yet. The prophet Habakkuk said:

> This vision-message is a witness
> pointing to what's coming.
> It aches for the coming—it can hardly wait!
> And it doesn't lie.
> If it seems slow in coming, wait.
> It's on its way. It will come right on time.
> —Habakkuk 2:3, The Message

Sometimes you have to do like church folks did in the old days— you "tarry" until He gives you what you need. You wait patiently, faithful to the vision He has already given you even as you seek for more vision. The apostle James wrote, "Draw nigh to God, and he will draw nigh to you" (James 4:8, KJV). Jesus said, "Seek first the kingdom of God and His righteousness, and all these things shall be added to you" (Matt. 6:33).

This waiting/seeking thing seems to be one of the most basic principles in the kingdom of heaven. You may feel like you're doing nothing. You may feel like you're in kindergarten. But hey, there's nothing wrong with kindergarten! The Bible says, "Do not despise these small beginnings, for the LORD rejoices to see the work begin" (Zech. 4:10, NLT). You *will* grow. And the person who has already gone on up to a higher "grade" needs to wait and seek some more in order to grow too. The thing about God is that He keeps beckoning you, "Come up higher. Come up higher!" That's all well and good, but the glorious problem is this: just when you think you are about to get to that point where you have finally reached your place in God, He moves on you and takes you higher still.

All you need to start with is your mustard seed of faith. Just get away to your place with God and plant that seed. It will start growing steadily. Take care of it and keep waiting for it to grow to full maturity.

KEEP STEADY

You may not seem to be moving very fast, and you may not seem to be attaining anything. But are you keeping steady? Are you keeping your priorities straight? Another key to successful pursuit is simply staying strong and steady, managing your ordinary, daily affairs with balance and wisdom.

Your moments will never defy your priorities. If you are married, for instance, the Holy Spirit will not tell you to abandon your covenant relationship in favor of becoming an itinerant evangelist. If you have a burning desire to become an evangelist, ask Him what to do with that. Don't rush into something if it makes you trample on your obligations.

Do you have children? Are they still young or are they older? Are you single? Do you have the responsibilities of a job or a ministry or going to school? Are you so busy that you sometimes feel like you should tell people, "Take a number, please!"

Ask Jesus to steer it all. Seasons come and go. Trust God with your timing. He can put people in your life who can move you to your next place. You may not be able to see them now, but He can raise them up. He can change your priorities if He needs to, although the best idea is to continue balancing your current priorities to the best of your ability in God's grace. He can also change your heart, shifting it to match the moment that's still out of the range of your sight.

Whatever you do, don't get stagnant. Don't settle for an existence instead of a life. Weigh and measure. Evaluate and ponder. Trust and obey.

REMEMBER THE SEEK-ADD PRINCIPLE

Don't forget Matthew 6:33: "Seek first the kingdom of God and His righteousness, and all these things shall be added to you." I love this because my husband calls it the "seek-add principle." In other words, if you seek, He will add. If you seek Him first—seeking His kingdom and His provision first—I promise you that He is going to add to you everything you need, in His time.

If you want more authority, more anointing, more power, the only place you're going to get it is from Him. It's not a vitamin. It's not even in His Word, apart from the breath of His Spirit. You won't find it in that anointed minister whose church you belong to (although you can seek better if you are around people who are also seeking His face).

Seek Him and then keep seeking Him some more. You will find that the saying is true: "Iron sharpens iron" (Prov. 27:17). Other people's anointing will rub off on you, as well as their fervent hunger for God. If you are seeking healing and a gift of healing, get around a powerful minister who has the gift of healing. If you want to become a better worshiper, get around someone who leads worship with true anointing.

Seek God relentlessly, with all the persistence you can muster out of your spirit. Keep asking even when God's answer seems to be no. The asking is supposed to be continuous. It's not a one-time thing. Jesus used a continuous action verb when He talked about it:

Keep on asking and it will be given you; *keep on seeking* and you will find; *keep on knocking* [reverently] and [the door] will be opened to you. For everyone who *keeps on asking* receives; and he who *keeps on seeking* finds; and to him who *keeps on knocking*, [the door] will be opened. Or what man is there of you, if his son asks him for a loaf of bread, will hand him a stone? Or if he asks for a fish, will hand him a serpent? If you then, evil as you are, know how to give good and advantageous gifts to your children, how much more will your Father Who is in heaven [perfect as He is] give good and advantageous things to those who *keep on asking* Him!

—Matthew 7:7–11, AMP, emphasis added

Jesus wants us to *keep asking without giving up*, just as my daughter Kaylee did when she was about nine years old. She came to Jamie and me and said, "Mom and Dad, I want a cell phone for Christmas." I couldn't believe that this child was asking for a cell phone at the age of nine. I'm almost fifty years old and I've had a cell phone for maybe three years. What does a nine-year-old need a cell phone for? We just said, "No, Kaylee, you are too young for a cell phone."

But Kaylee wouldn't give up. She kept coming to me, asking, "Mom, I want a cell phone. I really need a cell phone. My friends in school all have cell phones. Joshua has a cell phone."

I replied, "Kaylee, not *everybody* has one. And if Joshua has one, that's between him and his mama. You're too young to have a cell phone."

"Well, Mom, not everyone has one, but a lot of them do."

"No, Kaylee, we're not getting you a cell phone."

Then she goes back to her dad. "Dad, I really want a cell phone for Christmas." Of course her dad tells her to talk to me. So she came back to me and kept asking. "Mom, I want a cell phone..."

She kept on asking and asking, seeking and seeking, knocking and knocking.

You have to understand that this daughter of ours is a beautiful young lady. She loves Jesus with all of her heart. She's filled with the Spirit. She loves her mommy and daddy. She's very obedient. She's a straight-A student. She and her sister are both very well mannered and disciplined. (She's all that—and a bag of chips with a Diet Coke, thank you very much!) She is also very persistent!

This asking thing started to get to me. I started to think about it. "Wow, wouldn't it be great if she did have her own cell phone? When I'm away from home, I could call her. I could hear her sweet voice immediately instead of hearing the voice of the caregiver."

You know what happened? Christmas finally came. Kaylee got her cell phone.

You have to pursue God as Kaylee pursued her parents. Press in, asking Him all the time for everything that He says you can have. That's the seeking and asking and knocking. If you do that, He will answer you. You will find, and you *will* receive.

NEVER GIVE UP

The writer of the Book of Hebrews summed up a lot of what I'm trying to say when he wrote:

> Without faith it is impossible to please Him, for he who comes to God must believe that He is, and that He is a rewarder of those who diligently seek Him.
>
> —Hebrews 11:6

Did you get that last part? He rewards those who *diligently seek* Him. The word *diligently* implies persistence, never giving up. You have to keep on keeping on. Without diligence and perseverance, you will not succeed.

In Greek, the phrase "diligently seek" is from the word *ekzeteo*. Dr. Rick Renner, a Greek scholar and pastor/evangelist who has an international ministry, helped me to understand the full meaning of this word:

> The phrase "diligently seek" in Hebrews 11:6 is taken from the Greek word *ekzeteo*, and it carries an entire range of power-packed meanings. It means "to zealously seek for something with all of one's heart, strength, and might." It presents the picture of "one who seeks something so passionately and determinedly that he literally exhausts all his power in his search."
>
> Because the word *ekzeteo* portrays such an earnest effort, the idea of being hard working, attentive, busy, constant, and persistent in one's devotion to what he or she is doing is also included.
>
> This tells us that Hebrews 11:6 means: "God is a rewarder of those who put all their heart, strength, and might into seeking Him. Those who are so committed in their search that they are willing to exhaust all their natural powers in their search for Him—they are the ones who will find what they are seeking!"[3]

In order to seek God this diligently, you need supernatural perseverance. You need the kind of "stick-to-itiveness" that will not give up, ever. If you have this kind of determination, you will prevail. No obstacle will stop you. For members of the early church, this meant that no amount of persecution or hardship would deter them. They rejoiced and pressed on. They encouraged each other and persevered.

There is another Greek word, *hupomeno*, that conveys the meaning of what I'm trying to get across. The word is often translated "patience" in the King James Version of the Bible, and yet Renner says:

> A more accurate rendering would be *endurance.* One scholar calls it *staying power,* whereas another contemporary translator calls in *hang-in-there power.* Both of these translations adequately express the right idea about *hupomeno.* This is an attitude that never gives up! It *holds out, holds on, outlasts,* and *perseveres.*[4]

This kind of determined strength and effort will enable you to prevail over any circumstance or stress or pressure. Trials and tribulations seem endless when you're in the middle of them, but in due time they will end. Your season will change. Your effort will have been worth every drop of sweat and every sleepless night.

DEVELOP A PASSION FOR HIS PRESENCE

Speaking of sleepless nights, let's turn our attention back to the *passion* that simply has to be involved in your ongoing process of seeking God. As my mom did, sometimes you need to miss some sleep in order to seek Him. Jesus said, "Seek the kingdom" and "all these things" will be added to you. What does it mean to seek the kingdom of God? Is it as simple as seeking for an answer to a specific prayer, or is it bigger?

I believe that, first and foremost, it means seeking to be in His presence. This is not what most Christians in America want to hear. Fifty million people in this country are supposedly born again. But most of them view God in terms of what He can do for them. People want a God who will make them rich, happy, and comfortable.

Only rarely do they seek Him for Himself. They may not realize that they're allowed to ask God to manifest Himself—right where they are.

His presence can be a tangible thing. You may not always feel it, but you shouldn't rule feelings out. What we call "Holy Ghost goose bumps" may be just the beginning. When you really enter into His presence, you will never be the same again. That's what happened to Isaiah. Whether he was transported bodily to the throne room or he had a vivid vision, he was completely undone by the experience:

> GOD'S HOLINESS BECOMES AN ANOINTING ON SOMEONE LIKE ISAIAH, SOMEONE WHO HAS PURSUED GOD'S HOLY PRESENCE RELENTLESSLY AND WHO WANTS TO HELP BRING HEAVEN TO EARTH.

It was in the year King Uzziah died that I saw the Lord. He was sitting on a lofty throne, and the train of his robe filled the Temple. Attending him were mighty seraphim, each having six wings. With two wings they covered their faces, with two they covered their feet, and with two they flew. They were calling out to each other, "Holy, holy, holy is the LORD of Heaven's Armies! The whole earth is filled with his glory!"

Their voices shook the Temple to its foundations, and the entire building was filled with smoke. Then I said, "It's all over! I am doomed, for I am a sinful man. I have filthy lips, and I live among a people with filthy lips. Yet I have seen the King, the LORD of Heaven's Armies."

> Then one of the seraphim flew to me with a burning coal
> he had taken from the altar with a pair of tongs. He touched
> my lips with it and said, "See, this coal has touched your lips.
> Now your guilt is removed, and your sins are forgiven."
> Then I heard the Lord asking, "Whom should I send as a
> messenger to this people? Who will go for us?"
> I said, "Here I am. Send me."
> —Isaiah 6:1–8, NLT

Isaiah was a prophet, probably one of the greatest prophets of Israel. He spoke for the King of kings to the king of Israel and to the people of Israel. He had many notable moments in his long career because he served as a prophet for sixty years under four different kings. Good King Uzziah had reigned for fifty years, and he brought peace to the people. When he died, panic set in, and the people were fearful. But Isaiah set his heart on the presence of the King of kings. He pursued the presence of God as he had always done, only now with more passion.

He knew, of course, that God is holy. But he did not really know *how* holy God was until he was taken to the throne room. There, in God's presence, Isaiah couldn't even stand up. He felt filthy, unclean, unholy, unworthy. He was completely overwhelmed. He felt like he was going to die.

Isaiah was ruined. He had sought for the presence of God with a prophet's passion, but now that he was in God's presence, he was in no condition to do anything about it. He couldn't even say "Holy, holy, holy" like the seraphim. Facedown on the floor, he couldn't even think.

But then the angel came up to him and cleansed his lips. He became capable of responding to God's invitation. He had what he needed. He could now head out to preach and teach and proclaim the kingdom of God to the people of Israel, endued with a power that he had never experienced before.

God's holiness becomes an anointing on someone like Isaiah, someone who has pursued God's holy presence relentlessly and who wants to help bring heaven to Earth. God's presence stays with a person, as it stayed with Moses when he came down from the mountain and the people begged him to veil his face because it was so bright (Exod. 34).

Develop a passion for His presence. Seek His face. He will be found by you—and you will be changed into the person He wants you to be, bold and decisive, faithful and fruitful.

FIND YOUR CALLING

As you pursue God, you can expect God to show you what He wants you to do. He may not call you to preach to the nations of the earth, but rest assured that He will call you to do something for which you are equipped and motivated—something that you will be excited to undertake. Regardless of how difficult it is, you will be glad to do it, because your calling will fit you perfectly.

In the fifties in the United States, there was a healing movement and many anointed men and women of God rose up—men like Oral Roberts and women like Kathryn Kuhlman. In the sixties, there was a movement that was centered around the Word of God. The Word was preached with power and insight. The seventies saw the rise of the charismatic movement in the body of Christ. The Holy Spirit was no longer confined to a few churches and individuals, but He was poured out on men and women from many nations and denominations. In the eighties, we saw a move of miracles, signs, and wonders. And in the nineties, we saw an amazing move of revival and passion for God.

Now we are looking around and wondering what God will do in the first part of the twenty-first century. Who will the big names be? Whose church will become a household word? Instead of famous names and places, what we're seeing is a movement among ordinary people. Ordinary men and women of God are pursuing Him with unreserved passion, and they are stepping into callings that are distinctive. I believe this is "the saints' movement."

In the saints' movement, ordinary believers give themselves to God and He shows them specific callings. I'm talking about people God will use in the marketplace, in the grocery store, in Wal-Mart. These are people who are called to minister within the school system or in government.

These people know that they are part of a body. They know they are not one-man shows. They possess an increasing amount of divine authority and a greater boldness than they had before. They have tasted the glory of God, and they are consumed with a passion for Him. They carry specific anointings, and their prayers are powerful. These people know that they belong to a God who has made covenant with them.

You are part of this generation, and you can be sure that He will fulfill His part of the bargain where you are concerned. "God, who began the good work within you, will continue his work until it is finally finished (Phil. 1:6, NLT). In Philippians, we also read, "God is working in you, giving you the desire and the power to do what pleases him" (Phil. 2:13, NLT).

He is always working in us, and it is always good. He is doing a specific work in you. It's an anointed, chosen work. God saw you even before you were born, and He gave you a destiny. He gave you a compass for your life, even when you were still in your mother's womb. As you pursue Him, He will reveal your destiny to you, and you will begin to walk it out even as He shows you the next step.

In addition, He will supply you with everything you need to fulfill your destiny. Do you need confidence? He'll give that to you. Do you need creativity? Boldness? Endurance? Love? He's the source for every good thing. Do you need money? Do you need friends? Mentors? He can bring them into your life as well. (I will say a lot more about the importance of mentoring in the eighth chapter of this book.)

Your God is Jehovah-Jireh ("The Lord will provide"). He is a God who sees your needs and provides for them. He knows the destiny He has established for you, and He doesn't forget about it. He is Jehovah-Nissi ("The Lord my banner"). He is Jesus, your Savior, and He is Adonai, your Lord and God. Praise His name forever!

It's Time!

You need to become convinced, if you aren't already, that it's time for you to act. You can expect to see an acceleration in your prayer, a greater intensity in your anointing, and much greater boldness and perseverance that come straight from God. You can expect to grow in your God-given authority, resulting in an aggressiveness in the spirit realm.

I want to close this chapter with a true story. It will sound familiar to you, and yet it will seem fresh if you read it while thinking of the words *don't miss your moment*!

Jesus, worn out by the trip, sat down at the well. It was noon.

A woman, a Samaritan, came to draw water. Jesus said, "Would you give me a drink of water?" (His disciples had gone to the village to buy food for lunch.)

The Samaritan woman, taken aback, asked, "How come you, a Jew, are asking me, a Samaritan woman, for a drink?" (Jews in those days wouldn't be caught dead talking to Samaritans.)

Jesus answered, "If you knew the generosity of God and who I am, you would be asking me for a drink, and I would give you fresh, living water."

The woman said, "Sir, you don't even have a bucket to draw with, and this well is deep. So how are you going to get this 'living water'? Are you a better man than our ancestor Jacob, who dug this well and drank from it, he and his sons and live-stock, and passed it down to us?"

Jesus said, "Everyone who drinks this water will get thirsty again and again. Anyone who drinks the water I give will never thirst—not ever. The water I give will be an artesian spring within, gushing fountains of endless life."

The woman said, "Sir, give me this water so I won't ever get thirsty, won't ever have to come back to this well again!"

He said, "Go call your husband and then come back."

"I have no husband," she said.

"That's nicely put: 'I have no husband.' You've had five husbands, and the man you're living with now isn't even your husband. You spoke the truth there, sure enough."

"Oh, so you're a prophet! Well, tell me this: Our ancestors worshiped God at this mountain, but you Jews insist that Jeru-salem is the only place for worship, right?"

"Believe me, woman, the time is coming when you Samari-tans will worship the Father neither here at this mountain nor there in Jerusalem. You worship guessing in the dark; we Jews worship in the clear light of day. God's way of salvation is made available through the Jews. But the time is coming—it has, in fact, come—when what you're called will not matter and where you go to worship will not matter. It's who you are and the way you live that count before God. Your worship must engage your spirit in the pursuit of truth. That's the kind of people the Father is out looking for: those who are simply and honestly themselves before him in their worship. God is sheer being itself—Spirit. Those who worship him must do it out of their very being, their spirits, their true selves, in adoration."

The woman said, "I don't know about that. I do know that the Messiah is coming. When he arrives, we'll get the whole story."

"I am he," said Jesus. "You don't have to wait any longer or look any further." Just then his disciples came back. They were shocked. They couldn't believe he was talking with that kind of a woman. No one said what they were all thinking, but their faces showed it.

The woman took the hint and left. In her confusion she left her water pot. Back in the village she told the people, "Come see a man who knew all about the things I did, who knows me inside and out. Do you think this could be the Messiah?" And they went out to see for themselves.

—John 4:6–30, THE MESSAGE

You know, Jesus must have reported this conversation to His disciples, word for word, because when He was talking with the woman, the disciples were not with Him. I don't think Jesus told them everything just because He needed to show off His prophetic gifting. I think He wanted them to see how eager He is to be involved with each of us, even with those of us who think we're disqualified. He'll go out of His way to find a way to do it. He'll disregard unusual and difficult circumstances, and He'll make sure that as many other people as possible can have a moment with Him as well.

With God, you never know what's going to happen! It's worth anything and everything to encounter Him. Pursue God. You know that at the end of your pursuit, there is a prize. God will hear you, and He will come to you in a moment. Each of your God moments is stored up for you, waiting for the right time.

There's no turning back. Paul said:

> One thing I do, forgetting those things which are behind and reaching forward to those things which are ahead, I press toward the goal for the prize of the upward call of God in Christ Jesus. Therefore let us, as many as are mature, have this mind; and if in anything you think otherwise, God will reveal even this to you.
>
> —Philippians 3:13–15

CHAPTER 3

EXPECTING THE UNEXPECTED

THE GOD OF Israel had always done unusual things, and Ezekiel was a prophet, so he was used to it. But what happened to him one day must have taken him by surprise. There he was, just minding his own business, doing whatever Old Testament prophets did when they weren't busy prophesying. All of a sudden, "The LORD took hold of me, and I was carried away by the Spirit of the LORD to a valley filled with bones. He led me all around among the bones that covered the valley floor. They were scattered everywhere across the ground and were completely dried out" (Ezek. 37:1–2, NLT).

Ezekiel didn't even know where he was. God just snatched him up and took him to this desolate desert valley where the landscape was strewn with human bones. He seemed to have landed in a huge desert cemetery. Even if God had told him about it ahead of time, I don't think Ezekiel would have been able to believe it.

Those bones weren't only dead. They were bleached white, dried out, *old*. Those bones were deader than dead, and they were drier than dry. They weren't even connected together anymore into skeletons. They were just scattered and piled, sticking up every which way. I've never seen such a sight, and I'm sure you haven't either. Ezekiel just stood there in the hot wind, staring.

Then, over the howling of the wind, he heard God's strong voice: "Son of man, can these bones live?" (Ezek. 37:3). What kind of a question was that? They were so dead the flies weren't even interested in them anymore. The situation was obvious, wasn't it? And yet Ezekiel knew his God could do anything and that He often did what you would least expect.

So Ezekiel gave the only answer he could think of: "O Sovereign Lord, you alone know" (Ezek. 37:3). God must have thought that was a good answer, and He took it from there. He started to give Ezekiel directions, and Ezekiel did what he was told to do. Step-by-step, bone-by-bone, hundreds of dead bodies were reassembled, fleshed out, resurrected. Soon an army of living, breathing, strong men was assembled on that valley floor. There was not a single spare bone to be seen anywhere.

> SMALL, NEEDY
> BEGINNINGS CAN
> LEAD TO COMPLETE,
> SPECTACULAR
> FULFILLMENT.

Sometimes you and I are something like Ezekiel. We are just going along, living our normal lives. Then there's some kind of a turn in the road, and things get really desperate. There you stand, staring at a serious mess. You've never faced such a thing before. Is this a nightmare? But you're not asleep. Then God speaks up, "Son, can this marriage live?" "Daughter, can your children be saved?" "Child, can you survive?"

Like Ezekiel, you can answer only one thing: "Lord God, You know." And you will wait for whatever He might say next so that you can respond to it. You know your God can work miracles. Maybe this time you're about to see one. You know it might be a process, and it might take awhile, but you are willing to step out and obey. You're willing to be uncomfortable, and you don't mind if you have to work hard. You're full of faith. You know that your God is with you. Because you *know* what kind of a God He is, you've seen Him work many times in your life, and this is no exception. That's why you are able to walk into the unexpected, whether it's good or bad. You've learned *not* to rely on your own eyes and ears or your own limited human understanding. You have learned to expect the unexpected.

STARTING SMALL

I'm sure you have heard the advice: "Despise not small beginnings." (See Zechariah 4:10.) It means that you shouldn't underestimate something that doesn't look like much—yet. Everything that now looks spectacular started out small. The whole world, for instance, is a good example of this. This mighty Creator God can make things out of nothing. It's His specialty. Nothing is too hard for Him.

So, in a way, there's nothing surprising about the way He made the dry bones live. He's still doing the same thing when He takes a life that has been ruined and pulverized into dust—and He makes it new! It doesn't matter that that life (or marriage or family) is *not* whole and healthy and that it has been beaten apart into nothing more than a pile of little, tiny pieces. Even though those beat-up fragments appear to be too small to become the beginning of anything good, they can and they will rise again into life—if the sovereign God says so. Small, needy beginnings can lead to complete, spectacular fulfillment.

In other words, your "moment" may not look like much, but it may lead to something big. When I started singing, I didn't start at big churches, big conferences, or on satellite TV singing to millions. I started with my sisters, singing bed to bed in hospitals, going from cell to cell in jailhouses, or getting up early in the morning to sing at my school chapel services. Anyplace I had a chance to sing, I was glad to do it. It didn't matter whether I got paid or not. My sisters and I used to pray that we'd get enough of an honorarium to be able to get something to eat on the way home. Sometimes we did, and sometimes we didn't. Those were our days of small beginnings. If it was a really good honorarium, it was Shoney's for dinner. If it was a medium honorarium, it was McDonald's. If it wasn't such a good one, we'd be happy with crackers on our laps, and believe me when I tell you those were some of the most blessed times of my life.

I'm not trying to say that small beginnings always will lead to success and fame. They might or they might not. It could be that the main thing you're called to do for the rest of your life is to keep on going from bed to bed in a hospital, singing the gospel message to sick people. Your faithfulness will make you famous in heaven.

You can't tell ahead of time. Even if you are struggling through a terrible time and your hope is just about gone, God may show up when you least expect it and begin to turn things around. Remember that the Bible says, "…*with* God all things are possible" (Matt. 19:26, emphasis added). It's not "*to* God all things are possible." The Bible is clearly suggesting here that there is something that God expects out of us. It has to start somewhere, and it will probably start small. You'll wake up some morning with a little bit more faith than you had last night. You'll hear a faint word, and you'll be able to stand on it. You'll go out the door with a little more courage, and you'll turn right instead of left when you get to the street. Next thing you know, you'll be saying something or doing something unexpected—something you've never done before. Circumstances that appeared to be hopeless will start to shift. After a while, your heart will be singing a new song. Your God will never cease to amaze you.

Mother Teresa started out young and inexperienced, not drawing any attention to herself. She just started ministering to the street people in Calcutta, India. Most of them were near death. She and the women who came to help her just kept loving them and praying for them and soothing their wounds and easing them into death and comforting their families. After years and years of this, Mother Teresa won a Nobel Peace Prize. She started out in insignificance and ended up becoming a household name. She was quiet but determined. She obeyed God. She did what she knew she should do. And God did the rest.

EXPECTANT FAITH

If you don't want to miss your moment, you need to have expectant faith. If you don't have expectant faith yet, you need to at least have enough faith to expect to receive some. The Bible declares that everyone has been given "a measure of faith" (Rom. 12:3). That means everybody has it, so you just need to ask God to increase it as the disciples asked Jesus to do (Luke 17:5).

Oswald Chambers talks about it like this:

> At the most unexpected moments in your life there is this whisper of the Lord—"Come to Me," and you are immediately drawn to Him [Matt. 11:28]. Personal contact with Jesus changes everything. Be "foolish" enough to come and commit yourself to what He says. The attitude necessary for you to come to Him is one where your *will* has made the determination to let go of everything and deliberately commit it all to Him.

"…and I will give you rest"—that is, "*I will sustain you,* causing you to stand firm." He is not saying, "I will put you to bed, hold your hand, and sing you to sleep," But in essence, He is saying, "*I will get you out of bed*—out of your listlessness and exhaustion, and out of your condition of being half dead while you are still alive. I will penetrate you with the spirit of life, and you will be sustained by the perfection of vital activity."[1]

God is not trying to make it harder for you. He's not playing some kind of hide-and-seek game with you. He really *wants* you to have expectant faith. He wants you to trust Him with your whole heart. He knows what He intends to do in your life, and He doesn't want you to miss it.

> TAP INTO GOD'S STRENGTH. REACH UPWARD LIKE THE BRANCHES OF THE APPLE TREE. DRINK IN THE RAIN HE SENDS.

So, what is it that you have almost given up on? What do you least expect to change? Stir up your faith and walk back into it, expecting the unexpected this time. Expect your loved one to be saved. Expect the husband or wife you have prayed for to enter your life. Expect your business to catapult forward with new vitality and new ideas from God. Expect your intimacy with the Father to grow and to become more powerful.

FOR EVERYTHING, THERE IS A SEASON

Without question, the season of time you are in will merge into the next season of your life. The circumstances of this season *prepare a place* for your next season. "For everything there is a season" (Eccles. 3:1, NLT).

Everything in your life and mine falls into a time and a season, whether or not we are consciously aware of what that season is. What season are you in right now? What season will you be heading into next? Do you feel like you've been on "hold"? Are you in a bitter-cold winter and tired of waiting for the springtime? Instead of complaining and giving in to despair, *use* this valuable season you are in right now. Use it to let your roots grow down deeper than ever before. Tap into God's strength. Reach upward like the branches of the apple tree. Drink in the rain He sends (yes, even the rain that falls in fierce storms and hits you hard in the face). And when the sun comes out, bask in it. Before you know it, your faded blossoms will grow into ripe fruit, fresh for the picking.

Even Job, who had more troubles than any of us will ever have, eventually found himself moving back into a fruitful season again, and this time it was better than it had ever been before: "Now the LORD blessed the latter days of Job more than his beginning; for he had fourteen thousand sheep, six thousand camels, one thousand yoke of oxen, and one thousand female donkeys" (Job 42:12). His friend Bildad the Shuhite had speculated that "though your beginning was small, yet your latter end would increase abundantly" (Job 8:7), and it was true.

Ezekiel looked at the beaten-down situation of the people of Israel, and the Spirit inspired him to prophesy:

> But you, O mountains of Israel, you shall shoot forth your branches and yield your fruit to My people Israel, for they are about to come. For indeed I am for you, and I will turn to you, and you shall be tilled and sown. I will multiply men upon

you, all the house of Israel, all of it; and the cities shall be inhabited and the ruins rebuilt. I will multiply upon you man and beast; and they shall increase and bear young; I will make you inhabited as in former times, and do better for you than at your beginnings. Then you shall know that I am the LORD.

—Ezekiel 36:8–11

Only the mighty right arm of God can accomplish it. He alone turns the seasons. Daniel knew this well (I already quoted this in chapter 1, but I want to bring the point home to you). He proclaimed the truth when he said:

Blessed be the name of God forever and ever,
For wisdom and might are His.
And *He changes the times and the seasons;*
He removes kings and raises up kings;
He gives wisdom to the wise
And knowledge to those who have understanding.
He reveals deep and secret things;
He knows what is in the darkness,
And light dwells with Him.

—Daniel 2:20–22, emphasis added

THE BIRTHING ROOM

Another way to look at the seasons of our lives is to look at how an expectant mother goes through the nine-month season of her life before her new baby is born. You can apply this comparison to all of your newborn ideas and initiatives.

Here's how it works: First you conceive an idea, sometimes by prior planning and sometimes almost by accident. It takes root in you. You begin to ponder it and mull it over. It begins to have a life of its own. It grows. You're in a gestational season, and you're nurturing the new life within you every day as it grows.

Eventually, it's time for your baby vision to be born into the cold, cruel world. It's a risky moment. There in the birthing room, it's your time for giving birth. This experience isn't happening to someone else. You can't just sit back and watch it happen on a DVD. It's really happening to *you*. You have to see it through. You may need some assistance (but let me warn you to be aware of who is allowed to come into your birthing room). It may involve quite a bit of pain. But you're determined—your baby will be born today, no matter what it takes.

You see, when you are trying to birth an international ministry or deciding for the first time to start leading a Bible study in your home, there may be someone there to discourage you in the call of God, to try to take away the dream that He has put inside you. So when you are in your spiritual birthing room, you don't want anyone in your face telling you, "This is too hard for you. Give up. All of this pressing and pushing is really not that important. Just lie back and relax, rest. Don't be so serious about this thing."

Has this happened to you? Do you know what I'm talking about? Do you know what it feels like to conceive the idea in the first place and then to carry it in hiding for months (or years) only to have someone discourage you in it? That's why I am encouraging you to surround yourself with godly people who, like Issachar, "know the times and the seasons" and can help you walk through this time. They can get in your face and encourage you to press and to push. Go for it! Get it out! Birth it! At times, that can seem like an endless season of your life. Have you experienced the moment of birth yet?

Have you felt that thrill of joy and fulfillment and dread of fear—all at the same time—that happens to you in your birthing room?

Whether it's a far-reaching international preaching ministry or a humble neighborhood Bible study, it's still just a baby at this point, and you have a lot of sleepless nights ahead of you. But you did it! God gave you the seed, and you planted it. You carried it in your heart. You birthed this new creation, and now you are now going to pick it up and carry it until it can walk on its own.

Occupy Your Season

To state the obvious (because quite frankly, I need to hear this as well as you), you need to identify your season to the degree that you can and then make up your mind to live it to the fullest.

> God has put His anointing on you. He's put a call on your life, and this season is part of its fulfillment.

Don't just sleep through a season, which may prolong it indefinitely. We're cautioned against that in the Bible. Here's how Eugene Peterson put it in *The Message* version: "You're sons of Light, daughters of Day. We live under wide open skies and know where we stand. So let's not sleepwalk through life like those others. Let's keep our eyes open and be smart" (1 Thess. 5:6).

Don't get aggravated and agitated and waste your energy wishing you were in some other season. Matthew tells us, "So do not worry or be anxious about tomorrow, for tomorrow will have worries and anxieties of its own. Sufficient for each day is its own trouble" (Matt. 6:34, AMP).

Don't get confused about the season you're in and wish that you were in somebody else's season. The Bible says, "Each one shall bear his own load" (Gal. 6:5). Or as the New Living translates it: "We are each responsible for our own conduct." You're in a particular season at this particular time because God has positioned you there.

Maybe you're single and you'd rather be married. You say, "Judy, I would love to be married. I would love to have someone alongside me. I would love to have a mate." But this is your single season. This is where God has you. Occupy your single season. Don't despise the season that God has put you in right now. He has a timetable, and it's ticking along. It may not look like anything is changing, but the season is shifting even as you read this paragraph.

God has called you to occupy this particular season for some length of time. Go ahead and occupy it with your whole heart. You can't wait for the sweet by-and-by. You can't say, "Well, I'm going to wait until I get married, when I have children, when we get all settled down and fixed up—then I'm going to do things for God." No, don't act like you're half a person. You are a whole person right now. God has put a spirit of excellence inside you. He has put stamina and greatness inside you. He's put His anointing on you. He's put a call on your life, and this season is part of its fulfillment. You can't wait for two years down the road. You have to occupy this season that you're in right now. Paul said that if you are single, don't look to be married; and if you are married already, you can expect many trials. (See 1 Corinthians 7.)

Your season right now might be working in a homeless shelter. It may be working in a children's ministry or a singles' ministry.

It may be staying home and taking care of your children or your elderly mother. It may be singing on a praise and worship team. No matter what it may be, do it heartily as unto the Lord, and who knows, you may bump into your Boaz just as Ruth did.

When I was first sent to study music at Lee University, nobody knew me. I was just another student. I knew there was an anointing on my life to sing, but I never went up to somebody to say, "Hey, I'm pretty good. Do you know who I am? I am the anointed of God! Listen to me; this place is going to go up in smoke!" I didn't do that. I waited and worked for a long time. I prayed and fasted and studied and occupied my season of being in school and starting out small. It was good to do it that way, because I could grow my roots down deep.

I didn't want to miss my moment to sing in a more prominent way, but I knew I would never hit my moment if I didn't prepare first. For that very reason, I have always tried to occupy all the moments of each season of life that I have found myself in. The moment is up to God.

GET OUT OF YOUR COMFORT ZONE

If you're going to capture your moment and move on to the next season, you may well have to get out of your old comfort zone. You may have to do it many times over the years, as seasons and circumstances change.

You have to get away from people who are doing nothing and get around people who are doing what you want to do. You have to leave behind the people who aren't getting anything done and find some people who are accomplishing something great for God. If you're waiting for somebody to "discover" you, to show up at your door, and lead you to a season of success, forget it. Most of the time you have to trust God, step out, and find out for yourself. Sometimes you have to open the door yourself.

When you decide to open the door and get out of your comfort zone, you may get hit in the face with a blast of stormy wind. But don't let that stop you. You have to do something you've never done in order to have something you've never had. Ask God what He wants you to do next.

In all likelihood, He will want you to go out there and get around people who intimidate you to greatness. I love to get around people who make me want to study, pray, fast, and prepare myself more effectively. I don't do it to compete with them; I do it to find out what makes them tick. But most of all I do it because I am so hungry for more of God and His ways. When you get around these mighty men and women of God, don't be ashamed to ask them to give you advice. Sometimes they will be encouraging and sometimes they will critique you. Either way, they will intimidate you to greatness. Constructive criticism will cause you to become more creative, and you'll be able to grow some more. You'll be able to explore new opportunities.

There's no enemy as strong as the enemy that lives inside me. It swallows me up with insecurity and confusion, and it makes me want to stay safe in my bedroom instead of venturing outside to explore. We are all experts at getting comfortable and complacent. No progress is being made, but we don't care. We have our little setup, and we feel good about it.

But when your spirit starts to stir up within you about doing something new and different, you have to get up out of your easy chair and go out to *meet your next God moment*. The very fact that it involves some discomfort is helpful because we're all alike in that when we're a little uncomfortable, we'll listen to God better. Sometimes to be able to really listen to God and obey Him we have to get *really* uncomfortable. I'm telling you—it's worth it!

YOUR DESTINY IS CALLING

The word *destiny* is almost overused these days. But it's a good word and a true one. You have a destiny and so do I. God has a plan for each of our lives. We fit into His kingdom, and we have a purpose. Every one of us was put here on this planet to *do* something. Each one of us has a purpose and a destiny. We're supposed to do something here on Earth before we go to heaven.

Each one of us has strengths and weaknesses. God wants us to understand ourselves well so that we can learn to operate out of our strengths. He wants us to know what we have the ability to do—and what we don't have the ability to do. Often He wants to show us how even our weaknesses can be converted into strengths (2 Cor. 12:10). But of course we need to know what our weaknesses *are* before we can give them to Him in order for them to be turned into strengths that will bring glory to Him and to His kingdom.

> YOUR DESTINY IS BEING LIVED OUT EVEN AS YOU WORK TO ATTAIN IT.

You may already know many of your strengths and weaknesses. But as you pursue your destiny, you will discover more. You have to find out what it is that God has placed in your spirit and life. It doesn't have to be "spiritual." Maybe your strength is that you excel in business. Maybe you are a gifted fund-raiser. Maybe you're a natural when it comes to working with computers. Maybe you have been gifted to sing or to play a musical instrument. Your spiritual gifts may include helps or teaching.

Whatever your gifts and strengths are, you have to be fruitful with them. God told Adam and Eve to be fruitful. That's still what we're supposed to do. Adam and Even didn't use their strengths to launch a new TV station, but that could be what you are called to do in this time and place where you live. Be fruitful. Produce some fruit. Produce fruit, and then reproduce it. Each time it gets reproduced, it will get better if you keep evaluating it and submitting it to God. You will go from strength to strength if you're walking in Him (2 Cor. 3:18).

The question is, do we have the patience to wait for the working out of His plan in our lives? Will we fight for new territory and hold fast to what we have gained? Do we have what it takes to stand strong? You need to have the patience to wait and the perseverance to press forward. You need to respect God's timing and not rush on ahead of Him. You need to live a life of holiness and purity, empowered by the Holy Spirit. Do you have the right stuff inside you so that you can wait until "it" comes? Remember, for everything there is a time and a season.

Work and wait. Keep an expectant heart. Tell yourself, "I *will* succeed; I *am* blessed; I walk in abundance; my body is healthy; my children are saved; my husband is filled; my wife is filled." Nurture the hope that is in you. The same power that raised Jesus Christ from the dead dwells in you. Nothing is too big for you to conquer. Whatever it takes, do it.

Your destiny is being lived out even as you work to attain it. I can hardly wait to see what the Lord wants to do!

Fully Confident

In chapter 2, we talked about being confident that God will complete what He has started in your life: "I am certain that God, who began the good work within you, will continue his work until it is finally finished on the day when Christ Jesus returns" (Phil. 1:6, NLT). I hope you know that He is bigger than any barriers that get in your way, including the devil himself.

Sometimes there are demonic assignments that come against us, especially when you are just about to step into a new season of your life. They may come at you fast and furious. The devil gets a little desperate sometimes. He's a defeated foe, but he's still kicking.

But if you are well on your way toward your destiny, you can walk right past the devil. On your way by, why don't you take back anything he may have stolen from you? You can approach your circumstances full of confidence because you belong to the God of the universe, and you believe He hears you when you say something to Him. "How bold and free we then become in his presence, freely asking according to his will, sure that he's listening. And if we're confident that he's listening, we know that what we've asked for is as good as ours" (1 John 5:14–15, THE MESSAGE).

You can be fully confident because His promise to you is very much like the one He made to the children of Israel:

> For the Lord has multiplied you to become as many as the stars! And may he multiply you a thousand times more and bless you as he promised.
>
> —Deuteronomy 1:10, TLB

CHAPTER 4

PRAISE WINS THE BATTLE

I LOVE THE CIRCUS! I enjoy the whole carnival experience, and I especially love to have a ringside seat under the big top.

The most thrilling part for me is when the lion trainer walks into the ring with those huge lions and tigers. I have yet to see a trainer walk in there sheepishly or act afraid. He walks in with complete authority. He looks so sharp in his safari suit and tall boots, and he holds himself erect and strong with his whip in his hand. Sometimes I watch him more closely than I watch the big cats he has trained so well. They never step out of line as he puts them through their paces, and I love to watch him exercise his authority so well. But I'm always glad that I'm safely seated in the audience and not out there in the ring instead of him. Would I like to insert my whole head into a lion's big open jaws and pretend I'm dinner? Not on your life, thank you very much! I don't possess the authority (not to mention courage) I would need for that assignment.

However, my own life is a different story. When I walk into the ring with the devil—who is called "a roaring lion, seeking whom he may devour"—I am able to walk in with full authority, to the point that sometimes the lion ends up looking like a meek kitty cat. I am able to "resist him, steadfast in the faith" (1 Pet. 5:8–9). What's the difference?

The reason I have confidence in my authority over the devil is because I have confidence in Jesus. He has tamed the lion named the devil once and for all, and I belong to Him. I go into that ring with God the Father on my left side and Jesus the Son on my right. I have the Holy Spirit walking before me and behind me. I never go in all by myself. I know who is with me.

Everywhere we go, we each need to walk with that authority. You know, the devil definitely wants you to miss your moment. He wants to seize the authority you have in Christ Jesus so that you get attacked in the line of duty. He doesn't want you to advance. He exists to steal, kill, and destroy (John 10:10). He assailed Jesus, and he'll do it to you. But you can prevail. When the enemy attacks you and robs you of your faith, your peace, your joy, your health, and your family members, you can take it back by force. I'm sure of this because I believe what the Bible says: "From the days of John the Baptist until now the kingdom of heaven suffers violence" (Matt. 11:12). (The New Living translation reads, "…the Kingdom of Heaven has been forcefully advancing.") The violent take it by force. I'm sure of this because I've proved it over and over in my own life, and I've seen many others prove it too.

Once we become part of the kingdom of God, we can each

> DON'T HOLD BACK AND SAVE YOUR PRAISING FOR THE VICTORY CELEBRATION. INSTEAD, DECLARE THE HIGH PRAISES OF GOD THE WHOLE TIME YOU'RE ENGAGING THE ENEMY.

become a lion tamer. You and I have authority in Jesus, and when we raise our voices, we release it. Sometimes I go ahead and roar like a lion myself when I'm in the heat of the battle. Other times, all I need to do is nod my head or give a little flick to the tip of my whip (which is the same as the sword of the Spirit, which is the Word of God—Ephesians 6:17) to show the enemy who's boss.

Most of the time, all I need to do is praise the Lord to make the devil leave me alone. It's true that praise wins the battle—every time. Don't hold back and save your praising for the victory celebration. Instead, declare the high praises of God the whole time you're engaging the enemy. Worship and praise God in the thick of the battle. Praise Him even if you don't feel like doing it. Don't only praise God after the answer comes; praise God *until* the answer comes. Praise is our best weapon against our adversary the devil, that roaring lion.

THE DEVIL IS A LIAR

Repeat it after me: "The devil is a liar."

The devil is such a big liar that it is *impossible* for him to speak the truth. He may seem to be telling the truth because he's bringing up something that's really happening ("You're discouraged because your daughter is rebelling against you..."), but he always takes it too far and makes it into something false ("...so you should give up praying for her. The situation is hopeless.") He may quote the Bible, as he did with Jesus in the wilderness (Matt. 4), but he always misuses it somehow, and he always misquotes it. He twists it. He just cannot resist lying. That's why we call him the deceiver.

He lives to discourage you and to put you down. He interferes with everything. He steals what God wants you to have. The same moment that the Spirit comes to bless you, Satan comes too. He gets in your way and blocks you from doing what you want to do. Paul wrote to the church in Thessalonica, "We wanted very much to come to you, and I, Paul, tried again and again, but Satan prevented us" (1 Thess. 2:18, NLT).

The devil takes your circumstances and rubs your face in them. He tries to put you down so low that you don't even have the energy to look up. More than once, Paul and his co-workers had this experience, so they knew what it felt like. Paul wrote about it: "We were crushed and overwhelmed beyond our ability to endure, and we thought we would never live through it. In fact, we expected to die" (2 Cor. 1:8–9, NLT). But Paul didn't stop at that point. He went on to say that the experience was not wasted, because "as a result, we stopped relying on ourselves and learned to rely only on God, who raises the dead" (v. 9). It can be the same for us. The devil hasn't changed, but neither has our God. He is our mighty Rock, and we can run to Him.

The devil is both a liar and a thief. One of the tactics he uses against you is this: he steals your praise. It's one of the first things he does when he attacks you. He makes you forget all about praising God. He makes you forget what the Word of God says. You just want to sit around and think about nothing except the problem you are going through.

The devil whispers, "You're so depressed. It's just not working out, is it? You don't know the way out, and you won't be able to find it. You aren't anywhere near a victory. The best thing to do would be to sit down. Better still, lie down. Now you're really *under* the circumstances, aren't you? I think I'll just take a seat on your back."

Hey, stop! Wait a minute! Strong warriors don't lie down in the middle of the battlefield. They stand up and fight. They get back up every time they go down. They get up and they keep standing for as long as it takes to win the battle. They fight back against whatever the enemy throws at them. Even if they get injured, they hold their ground. When the battle turns in their favor, *they* get to be the ones with their foot on the enemy's neck.

They keep praising God, no matter what they're going through. In the thick of the battle they make declarations such as:

"The Lord is on my side! I am not afraid."

"I'm going in! I'm going over! I'm going to win."

"I'm delivered. I'm set free!"

"I'm the head, not the tail!"

They're loud about it. They aren't afraid to open their mouths and declare the truth. They know that their voice represents their authority, and they won't let the devil knock them around.

They are tireless. They open their mouths and begin to declare how strong and invincible their God is. They thank Him and praise Him for being the One who has already vanquished every enemy, including death. They cry out with a loud voice, and they slash out with the sword of the Spirit, which is the Word of God. They say, "Do not rejoice over me, my enemy; when I fall, I will arise; when I sit in darkness, the LORD will be a light to me" (Mic. 7:8).

The saints of God shout God's praises until they have become obnoxious to the enemy. The devil cannot tolerate Jesus's mighty name. He *hates* to hear His name praised. After a while, he takes his demons and he flees. He says, "This is not worth it. I can't prevail here. I'm going to leave."

The Bible says:

O evil man, leave the upright man alone and quit trying to cheat him out of his rights. Don't you know that this good man, though you trip him up seven times, will each time rise again?

—Proverbs 24:15–16, TLB

Praise the LORD, who is my rock.
He trains my hands for war
    and gives my fingers skill for battle.
He is my loving ally and my fortress,
    my tower of safety, my rescuer.
He is my shield, and I take refuge in him....
Open the heavens, LORD, and come down.
    Touch the mountains so they billow smoke.
Hurl your lightning bolts and scatter your enemies!
    Shoot your arrows and confuse them!
Reach down from heaven and rescue me;
    rescue me from deep waters,
    from the power of my enemies.
Their mouths are full of lies;
    they swear to tell the truth, but they lie instead.
I will sing a new song to you, O God!
    I will sing your praises with a ten-stringed harp.
For you grant victory to kings!

—Psalm 144:1–2, 5–10, NLT

Those who trust in, lean on, and confidently hope in the Lord are like Mount Zion, which cannot be moved but abides and stands fast forever.

—Psalm 125:1, AMP

That makes me want to shout *hallelujah*!

THE DEVIL IS A FAITH STEALER

When the devil takes your praise, he steals your faith. It doesn't take long before he has also taken your healing, your financial provision, your friends and family, or whatever it was that you had faith for.

How are you going to get your faith back? By using the Word of God as a sword again. Pull that sharp sword out of its sheath, and let the light glint off it! Find out what the Word says about your situation, and wield it against your foe.

Are you sick? What does the Word say about your sickness? Does it tell you to crawl off in a corner and be miserable? I'll tell you what it says. Isaiah and Peter and many others proclaimed the truth:

> But He was wounded for our transgressions, He was bruised for our iniquities; the chastisement for our peace was upon Him, and by His stripes we are healed.
>
> —Isaiah 53:5

> He personally carried our sins in his body on the cross so that we can be dead to sin and live for what is right. By his wounds you are healed.
>
> —1 Peter 2:24, NLT

> Behold, I will bring [the city] health and healing; I will heal them and reveal to them the abundance of peace and truth.
>
> —Jeremiah 33:6

> God anointed Jesus of Nazareth with the Holy Spirit and with power. Then Jesus went around doing good and healing all who were oppressed by the devil, for God was with him.
>
> —Acts 10:38, NLT

Has the enemy been coming against your marriage, attacking you back and forth so that you've never seen such turmoil in your life? I'll tell you what to do: declare the Word of the Lord over your marriage, over your children, over your household. You'll see the power of the enemy dissolved. You'll see him conquered. You'll see God restore everything that the devil has snatched out of your hands. You'll see the power of the enemy destroyed in the mighty name of Jesus. Here is how God gives us His promise:

> So I will restore to you the years that the swarming locust has eaten, the crawling locust, the consuming locust, and the chewing locust, my great army which I sent among you. You shall eat in plenty and be satisfied, and praise the name of the Lord your God, who has dealt wondrously with you; and My people shall never be put to shame.
>
> —Joel 2:25–26

> The Lord will cause your enemies who rise against you to be defeated before your face; they shall come out against you one way and flee before you seven ways.
>
> —Deuteronomy 28:7

> Believe on the Lord Jesus Christ, and you will be saved, you and your household.
>
> —Acts 16:31

The Bible says, "The word of God is living and powerful, and sharper than any two-edged sword" (Heb. 4:12). God wants you to use it. He wants to convert your time of hardship into a moment of miraculous provision. Most of all, He wants to enable you to walk in faith again.

DON'T MISS YOUR MOMENT OF VICTORY

Don't miss your moment of victory. Picture yourself walking in victory. God told Joshua, "*See*, I have given you the city!" (Josh. 6). If you can see with spirit eyes in the supernatural, then you can believe for it to come forth in the natural. You have to *see* that drug-addicted, alcohol-drinking, carousing husband of yours filled with the Spirit of God and walking in truth and integrity and being the king, the priest, and the prophet of your home. You have to *see* that scraggly, rebellious teenager coming to her senses.

Can you see yourself walking in victory? What does it look like? Describe it out loud, and proclaim it in prayer, and then worship some more. Paul said to "fight," "press," "wrestle," "stand," and "keep the faith" (Eph. 6). As you do that, as Jesus did, you will begin to walk in joy, and God will set you in a place of honor, just as He did Jesus. Only by pressing through all the obstacles with loud worship will you get out of the wilderness you are in. When you worship, your weariness will disappear. It will be swallowed up in the glorious presence of God.

When you begin to worship God in spirit and truth and in total abandonment, it doesn't matter what kind of situation you are in—real, gritty, hurting. When you open yourself to God and worship Him in the thick of the battle, you will step into a new dimension of faith.

There is one thing about it though: you can't be up one day and down the next. You can't be believing one day and doubting the next. You can't say, "Glory to God. He's all sufficient, and He's going to help me" on Sunday and then on Tuesday say, "O Lord, woe is me. What am I going to do?" No, you have to hold fast to your profession of faith without wavering, for He who promised is faithful (Heb. 10:23).

James says:

> It must be in faith that he asks with no wavering (no hesitating, no doubting). For the one who wavers (hesitates, doubts) is like the billowing surge out at sea that is blown hither and thither and tossed by the wind. For truly, let not such a person imagine that he will receive anything [he asks for] from the Lord, [for being as he is] a man of two minds (hesitating, dubious, irresolute), [he is] unstable and unreliable and uncertain about everything [he thinks, feels, decides].
>
> —James 1:6–8, AMP

Begin to speak praise and confident faith to everything God has said. You have to speak faith into every vision that God has put inside of you.

When I say don't miss your moment, I'm telling you that this is your time and your season to reclaim all the territory the enemy has stolen from you. I think he's had it long enough, don't you?

Praise and Worship in Perilous Situations

The hardest situations call for the loudest praises. Oftentimes it's the praise that makes sure that you do not miss your moment. I believe that's what happened to Paul and Silas.

Paul and Silas were on one of their long mission trips. In Philippi, they had just cast the spirit of divination out of the slave girl, and as a result, they had been attacked and beaten by a mob led by her owners, who now could no longer earn money from her soothsaying.

> Then the multitude rose up together against them; and the magistrates tore off their clothes and commanded them to be beaten with rods. And when they had laid many stripes

on them, they threw them into prison, commanding the jailer to keep them securely. Having received such a charge, he put them into the inner prison and fastened their feet in the stocks.

But at midnight Paul and Silas were praying and singing hymns to God, and the prisoners were listening to them. Suddenly there was a great earthquake, so that the foundations of the prison were shaken; and immediately all the doors were opened and everyone's chains were loosed.

—Acts 16:22–26

Picture the two men: They were covered with bruises and welts from their beating, and they had been thrown into the inner prison, dark and windowless and crowded already with other prisoners, many of whom were true criminals. Their clothes had been ripped off, they were dirty and dusty, and they ached all over. They were exhausted from being dragged around and yelled at and beaten up, and they were hungry and thirsty. Besides all that, the jailer had locked their ankles into stocks so they couldn't get up and move around.

> TRUE WORSHIP CONVERTS *DOUBT* TO *DELIVERANCE*. IT CHANGES *UNBELIEF* TO *UTTER RELIEF*. PRAISE AND WORSHIP CHANGE *FEAR* TO *FAITH*.

Paul and Silas had been deprived of their freedom unjustly. No longer could they travel to the next town as they had planned to do. It was obvious that their lives were in danger, and who could say if any of their friends would be able to obtain their release? It would not be far-fetched to think that this was the

75

end of the road. They might just sit and rot here in this dark Philippian jail for the rest of their earthly lives.

What would you have done in that kind of a situation? Fret and worry and try to figure out how to hire a good lawyer? Would you sit around and moan and groan and talk about how hard it is to be in the ministry? Or would you have had a big all-night *hymn sing* as they did?

They might have been half dead, but their spirits were fully alive, and they weren't going to go quietly. They licked their cracked lips and opened their mouths and began to worship God in song, filling that dark and stinking place with the high praises of God. There is a time for silent prayer, but this wasn't one of them.

Some of us are too quiet in our prayer and worship. The devil wants to muzzle us. He tries everything (including, in Paul and Silas's case, slanderous accusations and beatings so severe that if they had occurred these days, Amnesty International would be on the case). But instead of shutting their mouths in total surrender, they chose to raise the volume of their praises. They didn't just sort of mutter their prayers as if they were ashamed of the gospel. They belted out those worship songs so loudly and so strongly that their fellow prisoners heard the good news that could set them free—literally, as it turned out.

It's as if the devil listened to the praises for a while along with the prisoners, but finally he could not stand it anymore. He left that prison in a hurry. In fact, he slammed the door so hard on his way out that it was like part of the earthquake! Paul and Silas and the others, including the jailer and his family, were all set free—all because of the bold, loud praises of two men who would not let the devil steal their praise.

BRINGING POWER TO YOUR PRAISE

Why are real praise and worship so powerful? What kind of a heavenly transaction goes on when we open our mouths and give God all the praises that are due to Him, whether or not we're stuck in some kind of a hopeless prison? I can think of five things that bring power to our praise.

1. Real worship releases a new dimension of faith.

The Bible says, "Faith without works is dead" (James 2:20, 26). The act of worship is a "work" that brings life into our faith. Praise puts legs under faith. And, as the writer of Hebrews pointed out, "without faith it is impossible to please Him" (Heb. 11:6). True worship converts *doubt* to *deliverance*. It changes *unbelief* to *utter relief.* Praise and worship change *fear* to *faith.*

2. Real worship changes the atmosphere.

You see it all the time. People straggle into a worship service tired and worn out. They may have come only out of a sense of duty. Then after only a few praise choruses, everyone starts to pull together. The atmosphere lightens up. It's like what happened to David in the course of a single psalm such as Psalm 22. He starts out in verse 1 lower than a snake's belly: "My God, My God, why have You forsaken Me? Why are You so far from helping Me, and from the words of My groaning?" By verses 3 and 4, he begins to perk up, praising his God because he has faith in Him: "But You are holy, enthroned in the praises of Israel. Our fathers trusted in You; they trusted, and You delivered them." By the end, he's saying:

I will praise you in the great assembly.
> I will fulfill my vows in the presence of those who
> worship you....
> All who seek the LORD will praise him.
> Their hearts will rejoice with everlasting joy.

The whole earth will acknowledge the LORD and return to
him.
> All the families of the nations will bow down before
> him.

For royal power belongs to the LORD.
> He rules all the nations....
> Future generations will hear about the wonders of the
Lord.

—Psalm 22:25–28, 30, NLT

3. Real worship will give grace and power to overcome any obstacle.

In the Bible, real military battles and real obstacles were overcome by the power of praise time after time. David, one of the greatest warriors of them all, put it into a psalm:

> I will bow down toward Your holy temple
> And give thanks to Your name for Your lovingkindness and
> Your truth;
> For You have magnified Your word according to all Your
> name.
> On the day I called, You answered me;
> You made me bold with strength in my soul.

—Psalm 138:2–3, NASU

4. Real worship will cause you to become a victorious warrior in the spirit realm.

Along with the verbal acts of worship, both spoken and sung, you will worship with your whole body. Your clapping and leaping and stomping carry the message of God straight to hell. Your shout of exultation will cause the walls of Jericho to come tumbling down. "Praise the LORD, who is my rock. He trains my hands for war and gives my fingers skill for battle" (Ps. 144:1, NLT).

Our old-timers had it right. They knew how to plead the blood of Jesus. I used to hear my mom do it all the time. At the mention of the blood of Jesus, your enemy trembles. He can't stand to hear about it. If only he had known how powerful it would be, he would never have crucified the Lord of glory. He would have left Him alone. He thought it would be like killing the babies before Moses or before Jesus. He thought death would be enough to stop God. Praise God, Jesus's death became the gateway to complete victory.

5. Real worship brings His presence.

By far the best thing of all is that true worship and praise usher in the King Himself. You will never miss the moment of His coming if you maintain a spirit of worship and praise.

> You who bring good tidings,
> Get up into the high mountain;
> O Jerusalem,
> You who bring good tidings,
> Lift up your voice with strength,
> Lift it up, be not afraid;
> Say to the cities of Judah, "Behold your God!"
> Behold, the Lord GOD shall come with a strong hand,
> And His arm shall rule for Him;

Behold, His reward is with Him,
And His work before Him.

—Isaiah 40:9–10

Talking to Yourself

Almost as good as praising the Lord aloud is talking to yourself aloud. Someone has said, "If you're not saying it, then you're not seeing it." David talked to himself. He said, "Bless the Lord, O my soul" (Ps. 103). He was talking to his own soul and telling it all the reasons it should get busy blessing the Lord:

Bless the Lord, O my soul;
And all that is within me, bless His holy name!
Bless the Lord, O my soul,
And forget not all His benefits:
Who forgives all your iniquities,
Who heals all your diseases,
Who redeems your life from destruction,
Who crowns you with lovingkindness and tender mercies,
Who satisfies your mouth with good things,
So that your youth is renewed like the eagle's.

—Psalm 103:1–5

David was telling himself to praise the Lord, who consistently provides such great benefits to His children. Forgiveness and healing and redemption and loving mercy and strength and all good things—that was just the beginning of his list. You know how easy it is to forget that these benefits come from God and how easy it is to forget to thank and praise Him for His goodness to us every day. David chose to remind himself of the truth so that his praises would come straight from his heart.

I talk to myself all the time. I pick myself up by the collar and look at myself in the mirror and tell myself the truth: "Girl, you know the truth, and the truth will set you free. Knees, stop quaking. There's nothing to be afraid of. God is on your side; He is your provider, and He will not abandon you. Stop acting like you don't believe it. Tell the Lord how much you love Him!" And then I start praising Him. My voice represents my authority, and it makes things shift in my favor.

Sometimes there's nobody around except you and God. But I tell you, you and God are a majority. If God be for me, who can be against me (Rom. 8:31)? Talk to yourself. Tell yourself, "I am anointed. I am appointed. I am called. I am coming out. I am going in. I am going over. I'm going to make it. The Lord is on my side. I know He is faithful and true."

The Bible writers knew the value and importance of opening their mouths to express what they knew to be true. They knew it wasn't enough just to "read silently" or to think about it (although that's good too, and there's nothing wrong with it). Notice the italicized word *say* in these verses:

> Let the weak *say*, "I am strong."
> —Joel 3:10, emphasis added

> Always be full of joy in the Lord. I *say* it again—rejoice!
> —Philippians 4:4, NLT, emphasis added

> Wait on the LORD;
> Be of good courage,
> And He shall strengthen your heart;
> Wait, I *say*, on the LORD!
> —Psalm 27:14, emphasis added

> I have not kept the good news of your justice hidden in my heart; I *have talked about* your faithfulness and saving power. I *have told* everyone in the great assembly of your unfailing love and faithfulness.
>
> —Psalm 40:10, NLT, emphasis added

> For You have delivered my soul from death,
> My eyes from tears,
> And my feet from falling.
> I will walk before the LORD
> In the land of the living.
> *I believed, therefore I spoke.*
>
> —Psalm 116:8–10, emphasis added

If you don't talk yourself into expressing your faith by praising God, you can't ever stand strong when storms hit. *Stand Strong* is the name of one of my books. The message of the book is summarized in Ephesians 6:10–13:

> Finally, my brethren, be strong in the Lord and in the power of His might. Put on the whole armor of God, that you may be able to stand against the wiles of the devil. For we do not wrestle against flesh and blood, but against principalities, against powers, against the rulers of the darkness of this age, against spiritual hosts of wickedness in the heavenly places. Therefore take up the whole armor of God, that you may be able to withstand in the evil day, and having done all, to stand.

That well-known passage goes on to describe the pieces of the armor of the Spirit, and I believe that all of them depend to a large degree on the intentional, audible declarations of our own mouths. Unless we talk about doing it, we cannot do a very good job of girding ourselves with truth; putting on our breastplate of righteousness, our shoes of the gospel of peace, or our helmet of salvation; or picking up our shield of faith or the sword of the Word (Eph. 6:14–17).

UNITED WITH OTHERS

When you stand strong, you stand united with your brothers and sisters in the Lord. You declare your faith to each other by both word and deed. Your unity spells defeat for the devil. He knows that one person alone can put a thousand to flight and that as few as two people, praying in agreement, can put ten thousand demons to flight (Deut. 32:30). He knows what happened at Babel (Gen. 11:7–9) when the people were building the tower with such unity that even the Father, Son, and Holy Spirit decided to come down and check things out. There was only one thing to do— confuse their languages, so they couldn't accomplish things quite so successfully:

> GOD took one look and said, "One people, one language; why, this is only a first step. No telling what they'll come up with next—they'll stop at nothing! Come, we'll go down and garble their speech so they won't understand each other." Then GOD scattered them from there all over the world. And they had to quit building the city. That's how it came to be called Babel, because there GOD turned their language into "babble." From there GOD scattered them all over the world.
> —Genesis 11:6–9, THE MESSAGE

United we stand, divided we fall. Unity is powerful. The devil hates it when the people of God are in unity and agreement. David said, "Behold, how good and how pleasant it is for brethren to dwell together in unity!" (Ps. 133:1) Who is it you call on when trouble strikes? I can almost hear someone say, "Jesus!" And Jesus is right. But let me assure you, most of the time it is going to be your pastor, your praying mother or grandmother, your prayer partner at church, or the person you sit beside in choir. You want somebody with some flesh on to agree with you, and rightly so. That's why Jesus set up the church. He knows the power when we pray together: "If two of you agree on earth concerning anything that they ask, it will be done for them by My Father in heaven" (Matt. 18:19).

God knows that whenever people can get together in unity, *anything is possible.* He wants to keep us unified with Him and with His body, the church. The enemy wants to belittle our efforts and tell us it's just not necessary. But God is looking for men and women and children who will dare to be different, who will open their mouths to declare their love for God and their love for each other.

Satan hates it when you worship together with other people, because it reminds him of what he used to experience in heaven. When he hears your worship, the devil has flashbacks of what it felt like to be in the awesome presence of God. It drives him crazy and makes him go away. He can't stand it. And that's the way we want it to be.

DEFEAT DISCOURAGEMENT

In this book, we've been talking about not missing your moment. We've been talking about finding your destiny and fulfilling it, step by step. We have to keep talking about this, because it really is possible to miss it. The devil knows that, and he's probably trying to distract you right now. He's interested in keeping you so distracted that you wouldn't recognize your moment if you tripped over it.

He wants you to be isolated and depressed and defeated. He wants you to think that your brothers and sisters can't help you. He wants you to forget about praising God. "God who? It's kind of hard to trust a God you can't see, isn't it?" he whispers to you. (Of course you can't see *him* either, but he doesn't bring that up.) The devil wants you to check out of the rat race, especially if you are starting to fulfill your calling in a ministry. He wants to keep you exhausted and confused, discouraged and puny.

I know this from firsthand experience. Sometimes I refer to it as a "fly spirit." Have you ever been trying to have a barbecue outside on your deck and this one fly just keeps circling around your head, getting on your hot dog, swarming around your potato salad, and you just keep swiping at it, hoping it will go away? That is the way the enemy is sometimes. He will send "fly spirits," something just to keep you annoyed and aggravated. You'll swipe here and swipe there to no avail. There is only one thing that is going to get rid of that fly—go get yourself a flyswatter and kill that thing. You have the power to kill that "fly spirit" coming against you with the Word of the Lord. Jesus said, "Behold, I give unto you power to tread on serpents and scorpions, and over all the power of the enemy: and nothing shall by any means hurt you" (Luke 10:19, KJV).

I can think of times in my ministry when I almost gave it all up. I was just barely making it. Once when I was single, I remember collapsing on the floor in my apartment. I wasn't exactly praying. I was crying and shaking my head and saying things into the air. My eyes were swollen, and my nose was so stuffed up I couldn't even breathe. I felt like I was down and out, lost and undone in a dying world. Like Elijah, I had just about decided that I was the only one living for Jesus, and certainly the only one suffering the way I was.

I ranted and raved to the Lord, "Here I am. You gave me this apartment, and now I can't even pay for it. I'm so hoarse from singing and preaching that I can hardly even talk to You." I was just a mess. I had just about had it with singing and preaching my heart out only to receive one of those "Sister Judy, what a blessing" offerings. I had hardly enough money to pay my bills, much less fulfill the dreams God had put inside my spirit. I figured I should just go back to my old job in a bank, or I could go to McDonald's and flip hamburgers.

> PRAISE IS OUR BEST INITIAL RESPONSE—AND OUR BEST CONTINUAL RESPONSE—WHEN THE DEVIL TRIES TO PLUNDER US.

I told God, "If You could just say one word to me, I'd appreciate it."

You know what He said? He said, "Get up and dance."

I thought to myself, "That isn't God. That is the devil making fun of me."

But God let me know it was Him: "This is Me. Get up and dance." So I got up on my knees, but I didn't dance.

God said, "Shout!"

I said, "God, surely You don't expect me to shout right in the middle of this mess I'm going through? Don't You know what's happening?"

All He said again was, "Dance."

And I said, "Lord, all my life I've tried my best to obey You. All my life I've tried to lift You up. I've tried to obey You in everything You've ever told me to do. And I'm going to do it now." I thought to myself, "Well, if I made it up to my knees, I reckon

I can get up on my feet." So I pulled myself up onto my feet. At first, all I could do was rock back and forth. Then I thought, "I'm not going to just stand here. I'm going to walk a little bit." So I started to walk a little bit.

Then I remembered that God had told me to shout. I croaked out, "Well, here I am, just going through all this. I just thank You, Lord, because You are my Savior. I just thank You for all You've already brought me through. I know You are making a way right now." I thought, "You know, that feels pretty good. I think I'll just lift my hand a little bit." So I lifted my hand. I got one hand up. I told Him He was my Jehovah-Jireh, my Provider, and that there was nothing too hard for Him. I told Him there wasn't anything I would ever face that He couldn't help me with.

Before I knew it, I had both my hands up and I *was* shouting with the voice I had left, dancing all over the place. Things were looking up. The devil had to excuse himself. He took that load of discouragement and he left. God's provision came first into my soul and spirit, and then for my circumstances.

GETTING THE HANG OF FAITH

God will never show you the end of your journey. You can't see it except maybe in the spirit realm. You know the general direction to take; you know it's over that hill ahead. To get there, you have get the hang of faith. You have to ride that baby like you're surfing. You have to ride it out. It may be a bumpy ride and you may fall off the side, but just keep holding on. Get back on again. Try again, even if the waves may swamp you.

Get busy doing what God has for you to do right now, because all of it is *preparation* for the *place* that He has *prepared*. Occupy the season you are in right now. Give God the glory right now. Praise Him and trust Him with every fiber of your being right now!

While I was preparing this chapter, I happened to receive one of Francis Frangipane's e-newsletters. In an article called "Rule in the Midst of Your Enemies," he wrote: "Before you go into warfare, recognize that it is not you that the devil is afraid of; it is Christ in you! We have been raised up and seated with Christ in heavenly places (see Ephesians 2:6). This is why the Holy Spirit continues to speak to us that worship of God is our first response in battle."[1]

Praise is our best initial response—and our best continual response—when the devil tries to plunder us. Don't let Satan interfere with your life of faith for another minute. Don't miss your moment to praise God and to receive His provision in the process. Remember:

> He who is in you is greater than he who is in the world.
> —1 John 4:4

CHAPTER 5

DO YOU THINK YOU'RE DISQUALIFIED?

I AM VERY MUCH a shy person. I really am. People who are close to me will tell you that it's true. But when I get under God's anointing, watch out! I'm wide open, and nobody in the room will even *think* the word *shy*.

When I was a little girl, if my mother and sisters hadn't persuaded me that God had called me to stand up in front and sing, I don't think I would ever have done it. But they knew that I had a call on my life, and they made sure I knew it too. They knew that my natural shyness did not mean that I was disqualified as a gospel singer. They knew the Holy Spirit would come in power and change shy little Judy into somebody who was bold and outspoken, somebody who would proclaim the gospel. They trained me to wait for God's power to come, and they trained me to count on it.

That's all that mattered then and it's all that matters now. God will supply everything that I need in order to do His will. My so-called "disqualification" of shyness became one of my greatest assets, because it made me lean harder on Him. God does not require that I change myself before I can stand before Him. If God needs to straighten me out in some way, He can do that, and He will do that. What God is looking for is a willing heart. The best candidate for God's grace is somebody who is not qualified in his or her own strength at all—and who knows it.

QUALIFIED TO RECEIVE THE HOLY SPIRIT

Who is "qualified" to receive the Holy Spirit? Nobody is. At the same time, *everybody* is.

In the Upper Room on the Day of Pentecost, not one person was qualified, and yet not one of them was disqualified. Every single one of them received the Holy Spirit that day. You would think that the only ones who would have had the right credentials might have been the eleven remaining disciples plus Matthias, who had replaced Judas. But they weren't the only ones in the room. We see in Acts 1:14 that right from the beginning they were joined by others: "They all met together and were constantly united in prayer, along with Mary the mother of Jesus, several other women, and the brothers of Jesus" (NLT). The next verse tells us that there were about one hundred twenty of them, both men and women, who stayed there together, praying and waiting.

> GOD WANTS TO USE YOU REGARDLESS OF YOUR AGE, YOUR APPEARANCE, YOUR EDUCATION, YOUR RACE, YOUR GENDER, OR YOUR PRIOR EXPERIENCE.

When the Day of Pentecost came, every single one of them was filled with the Spirit—no exceptions. Nobody went away empty, and nobody went home half filled. To receive the Holy Spirit, the same

Spirit that was in Jesus, the only two qualifications they needed were a wholehearted belief in their resurrected Lord and enough obedience to keep them waiting as He had told them to do. That's it. They didn't have to make a special pilgrimage or give away everything they owned or prove that they could perform amazing exploits or go without food. (Some of those things would come later, after the Holy Spirit had filled them.) They didn't have to hide away until their characters got purified and their sins disappeared. They just came as they were, without a lot of preparation, and they waited expectantly for the moment when God would fulfill His promise. Not one person was disqualified.

On top of that, the Jews who came running to the house when they heard the ruckus were not disqualified either. Every one of them heard the good news, regardless of their nationality or language, because the Holy Spirit made sure that each language was represented:

> At that time there were devout Jews from every nation living in Jerusalem. When they heard the loud noise, everyone came running, and they were bewildered to hear their own languages being spoken by the believers. They were completely amazed. "How can this be?" they exclaimed. "These people are all from Galilee, and yet we hear them speaking in our own native languages! Here we are—Parthians, Medes, Elamites, people from Mesopotamia, Judea, Cappadocia, Pontus, the province of Asia, Phrygia, Pamphylia, Egypt, and the areas of Libya around Cyrene, visitors from Rome (both Jews and converts to Judaism), Cretans, and Arabs. And we all hear these people speaking in our own languages about the wonderful things God has done!"
>
> —Acts 2:5–11, NLT

That same day, three *thousand* of them became full-fledged believers (Acts 2:41)! Again, no one was disqualified because of their sins or their shortcomings. A crowd of that size and from all of those places must have included every kind of person you can imagine. Some of them were probably big sinners. Undoubtedly, some of them had incurable diseases. A lot of them probably had what we would call today "relationship problems." Some of them drank too much. Some were lazy. Some were fat, and some were skinny. Some were introverts, and some were extroverts. Some were worriers, and others were careless. You get the idea.

It's beginning to look like no one is disqualified to meet up with God, no matter what the devil tries to make us believe.

Remember the Favor of God

One of the key words of my ministry is *affirm*. That's why I love this scripture, especially in the Amplified version:

> Arise [from the depression and prostration in which circum-stances have kept you—rise to a new life]! Shine (be radiant with the glory of the Lord), for your light has come, and the glory of the Lord has risen upon you!
>
> —Isaiah 60:1, AMP

God wants to use you as much as He wants to use me. He wants to use you regardless of your age, your appearance, your education, your race, your gender, or your prior experience. He never disqualifies you on that kind of a basis. He has given you gifts and strengths, and He can turn even your weaknesses into strengths. He replaces your fears with peace and your depression with joy. He changes your emptiness into fulfillment. He has given you a call and a destiny, and He will enable you to walk in righteousness so that you can accomplish it. As I have said already, He not only expects you to do His will, but also He is in you to do it.

Just when you think you must be the exception to God's favor because you can think of so many major disqualifications, He turns your face toward His so you can see the love in His eyes. "But Lord, I am not worthy. I'm not good enough. I didn't have the right daddy and momma; I don't know the right people; I'm too fat (or too skinny); I'm divorced and my kids are in trouble; I come from the wrong side of the tracks...."

He hushes your objections and reminds you of one thing: His *favor* rests on you. He has handpicked you every bit as much as He handpicked David to be the king of Israel. He's looking at your heart, and He's seeing somebody who can respond to Him. That's all He needs to see. "For the LORD does not see as man sees; for man looks at the outward appearance, but the LORD looks at the heart" (1 Sam. 16:7).

Too many people look at the outward appearance, just as Samuel looked at all of David's brothers. They were strong, handsome men. David was just a youth who probably couldn't even grow a beard yet. But he had the quality that God wanted. He was out there looking after his father's sheep, writing songs and singing them to God. It didn't matter that he was the youngest or the least in his family.

In the same way, the disciple Peter had to look past his preconceived notions about who was qualified to receive God's salvation. He thought it was limited to the Jews—and only to *good* Jews at that. But God showed him otherwise. He gave him the vision on top of the roof and then He sent him to Cornelius, who was a military officer who represented the nation that was oppressing Peter's fellow Jews. Much to Peter's amazement, God poured out His Holy Spirit on this Roman centurion and his non-Jewish friends just as generously as He had done for Peter and his Jewish friends. "Then Peter replied, 'I see very clearly that the Jews are not God's only favorites! In every nation he has those who worship him and do good deeds and are acceptable to him'" (Acts 10:34–35, TLB). Yes, He does!

How about you? Do you labor under a heavy load of preconceived notions about being unacceptable to God? Do you think your ordinary appearance or your limited intelligence or your humble pedigree is holding you back from receiving God's favor? Let the wind of truth blow away your own preconceived notions about your own worthiness or acceptability to God. Don't let something like that make you miss your moment.

What Are You Going to Do About It?

It's a lot easier to diagnose a problem than it is to fix it. If you can see some ways in which you have held God's blessings at arm's length because you felt you were disqualified, what are you going to do about it? I have some suggestions for you.

Take hold of grace.

First of all, you need to recognize that you need God's grace. God's grace will transform you. Every day, His grace will change you more into His likeness. It's a continual metamorphosis.

Each of us receives the gift of God's grace straight from Him. You don't have my grace, and I don't have yours. The Word of God says, "To each one of us grace was given according to the measure of Christ's gift" (Eph. 4:7). And like any gift, it needs to be *received* in order to be complete. The Giver holds it out; you need to accept it.

God's grace will make you able to function where He has established and destined for you to be in His kingdom. It will enable you to speak a word in due season to someone who needs to hear it. It will get you up and walk you through whatever circumstances you will have to face. Grace will empower you to do what you are called to do. It will make up for all your weaknesses. When the apostle Paul prayed that God would remove his thorn in the flesh, the Lord replied, "My grace is sufficient for you, for My strength is

> GOD IS BIG ENOUGH AND STRONG ENOUGH TO BRING YOU THROUGH SAFELY. SO WHAT ARE YOU WORRIED ABOUT?

made perfect in weakness" (2 Cor. 12:9). Minister Mike Murdock says it concisely, "The presence of God is the only place your weakness will die."[1]

But first you need to take hold of it.

> For the LORD God is a sun and shield;
> The LORD will give grace and glory;
> No good thing will He withhold
> From those who walk uprightly.
>
> —Psalm 84:11

Have a "different spirit."

You need to become like Caleb and Joshua, who had a different spirit from the rest of the Israelites who spied out the Promised Land. The others, you will remember, came back with a good report about the land itself ("it truly flows with milk and honey") but a bad report about what they judged to be the prospects of the under-equipped Israelites to conquer the "giants" who currently occupied the land. They reported that it was "a land that devours its inhabitants, and all the people whom we saw in it are men of great stature" (Num. 13:32).

Caleb and Joshua begged to differ. They were full of faith that they could indeed conquer that land and that God would help them win all the necessary battles. Even though their advice was outvoted, they hung onto their faith, and it was rewarded forty long years later when they were allowed to personally lead the next generation of Israelites into the Promised Land with success.

You need to have a Caleb-and-Joshua kind of spirit in order to prevail against the discouragement that is bound to come against you. You need to have a long-term, persevering kind of faith in order to make it. God is big enough and strong enough to bring you through safely. So what are you worried about? You don't want lack of faith to sideline you. Ask God for a different spirit—a faith-filled one.

God is looking for that different spirit in people. Paul told the church in Rome about it:

> This resurrection life you received from God is not a timid, grave-tending life. It's adventurously expectant, greeting God with a childlike "What's next, Papa?" God's Spirit touches our spirits and confirms who we really are. We know who he is, and we know who we are: Father and children. And we know we are going to get what's coming to us—an unbelievable inheritance!
>
> —Romans 8:15–16, The Message

This different spirit is the opposite of the spirit of fear. Fear makes us believe what we see with our eyes and it makes us doubt what we cannot see. Fear can occupy our minds and hearts so that we cannot take action. But God's perfect love can cast out fear. "God has not given us a spirit of fear, but of power and of love and of a sound mind" (2 Tim. 1:7). God's Spirit gives us a different spirit—if we will receive it.

Talk to yourself.

When I was a little girl, I used to talk to myself in the mirror. I used to sing to myself too. I'd get my hairbrush (for a microphone) and I'd go to town. I would sing in front of thousands and thousands of people, me and my hairbrush. It helped me gather together what I needed to go out there and do it for real.

I don't very often get my hairbrush and sing in front of my mirror anymore, but I do talk to myself in the mirror. I recommend it. I tell myself, "Straighten up. Listen here; do you know who you are? Do you know who God called you to be? Do you know how He equipped you? Now straighten up your shoulders and get up and go out there." I encourage myself like that. It helps.

Now if somebody would walk into the room, they'd think I was certifiably crazy; I know that. But I find that talking to myself makes me *less* crazy. It grounds me in the truth. It improves my character and deepens my integrity. It helps me live right and keeps me on track. I want to be holy and set apart for the Master's use, don't you? Go find your mirror and start talking to yourself!

King David didn't have a mirror, as far as I know, but he talked to himself too. We read in 1 Samuel that "David encouraged himself in the LORD his God" (1 Sam. 30:6, KJV). If it's good enough for King David, it's good enough for me.

Believe that God has made *you* righteous.

The apostle Paul was a mentor to a younger man named Timothy. A lot of his advice applies to the rest of us as well, such as the following:

> Pursue righteousness and a godly life, along with faith, love, perseverance, and gentleness. Fight the good fight for the true faith. Hold tightly to the eternal life to which God has called you.
>
> —1 Timothy 6:11–12, NLT

Paul wanted Timothy to believe the truth about himself, and the truth was that Timothy had been made righteous because he had responded to God's call. If you have responded to God's call, part of your ongoing response will be to believe that He has equipped you with every good thing that you will ever need. You are not disqualified because you feel insufficient. Regardless of how you feel about it, *He* is your sufficiency, so you are not insufficient at all.

Your flesh wants you to believe otherwise. Rick Renner writes:

> Left unchecked, your flesh will try to run you over, take charge of your emotions, and promote laziness in your life. It will tell you that you've done too much; that you've already done more than anyone else; that you don't need to do any more than you've already done; and that you're not as appreciated as you ought to be. Your flesh will advise you to kick back, take it easy, and cut yourself some slack....It's time to tell the flesh to shut its loud mouth! Then grab hold of the power of God to change you and the way you are thinking.[2]

Sinful nature always clings to the worst and to what is most negative. It will always gravitate downward, never upward. That is the nature of the mind that is not under the control of the Holy Spirit. If abandoned to your flesh, you'll never believe a good report; you'll never believe God is doing a good work in you; and you'll certainly never believe that you have been made "the righteousness of God in him" [2 Cor. 5:21, KJV].

Negative, base, sinful thinking has been a part of humanity for so long that it requires some special convincing to make us realize what God has done inside us. For us to really believe that we have right standing with God, it will take the work of the Holy Spirit to convince us! Otherwise, when God says, "You're my child. I have made you righteous. You are beautiful to Me," our negatively charged minds and emotions will retort, "It's not so! I'm unworthy. I'm unholy. I'm so pitiful."

...You don't have to be negative about yourself all the time. You don't have to beat yourself over the head, constantly reminding yourself of how unworthy you are, because Jesus made you worthy! He made you righteous![3]

You don't have to listen to your flesh, and you don't have to capitulate to the old, familiar lies that say you are disqualified. Jesus has set you free, and you can *choose* to believe the truth: you are righteous in Christ.

Call it into existence.

Sometimes you have to call a thing into existence. It's sort of like talking to yourself in the mirror, as I described above. You proclaim the truth into the atmosphere and you call forth those things that are not as though they were (Rom. 4:17). You speak "of future events with as much certainty as though they were already past" (Rom. 4:17, TLB).

You declare the truth about yourself; for example, "I am the called of the Lord. I have boldness. I have authority. I walk in the power of God. I walk in God's glory." You speak aloud the things that have been established in heaven so that they will come to pass in your human experience. You aren't waiting for pie-in-the-sky by-and-by. You are bringing it down into your life *today*. You are looking at the Word of God, turning its pages, reading aloud, and declaring its truth into your present-day existence.

As you proclaim it, you start walking in it. If you make an effort to speak it aloud, your proclamation makes a difference immediately.

Give it back to God.

Right away, as soon as you start to see results, you give everything back to God. He owns you and the results of your faith. Your job is easy. All you have to do is remember whose you are and let Him do things in you and through you.

> KEEP SERVING, KEEP BUILDING YOURSELF UP IN YOUR FAITH, AND KEEP ON ASSURING YOURSELF THAT IT'S WORTH IT, BECAUSE IT IS.

Be faithful to the "little" first. Do the thing He has set before you. The one hundred twenty believers who waited in the Upper Room just had to wait and pray. They had to stay in that room until they received power from on high because that's what Jesus told them to do. They had to sacrifice their time and just wait. For you, this will mean humble service. No limelight. Just roll up your sleeves and serve your heart out. Give everything back to God, and He will reward you in too many ways to count.

When I traveled with a group of singers, I was the lead singer, and nobody asked me to take other responsibilities on top of that. But somebody had to keep the bus clean, so I did. I think that kind of hard work gives glory to God, and He rewards it. Jamie and I tell our staff, "If you're working for us, you may get frustrated because you're not going to get a lot of attention, and you may not feel you are making enough money. You won't get accolades. But if you decide you're working for God, it will be different. You will enjoy working hard behind the scenes. And God will see it, and He will see to it that you are rewarded." Our ministry is a faith ministry, which means that it's a week-to-week ministry. We trust God every week for the bills and staff to be paid, and we try to bless our people as much as we possibly can. But ultimately, it's God who is providing the blessings. He sees the needs and rewards openly.

I know a doctor who sees patients four days a week, all day long. Then she comes in on her day off and vacuums, cleans the bathrooms, types, and does whatever needs to be done. She's a servant's servant. And because she is faithful over a few things, God gives her more blessings and more authority. You remember the ending of the story Jesus told. It goes like this:

> The master was full of praise. "Well done, my good and faithful servant. You have been faithful in handling this small amount, so now I will give you many more responsibilities. Let's celebrate together!"
> —Matthew 25:21, NLT

Never give up!

I've saved this simple advice for last because it needs to be said: never give up! You'll get tired, but don't let that stop you from keeping on with God. Don't disqualify yourself. Keep doing the good things God has taught you. Don't take a break from God. Paul exhorted the Corinthian church to keep running the race that was set before them so that they would not disqualify themselves:

> Do you not know that in a race all the runners run, but only one gets the prize? Run in such a way as to get the prize. Everyone who competes in the games goes into strict training. They do it to get a crown that will not last; but we do it to get a crown that will last forever. Therefore I do not run like a man running aimlessly; I do not fight like a man beating the air. No, I beat my body and make it my slave so that after I have preached to others, I myself will not be disqualified for the prize.
>
> —1 Corinthians 9:24–27, NIV

When you watch a race on TV, it may look exciting. However, you aren't the one out there running your heart out. You aren't the one out there sweating and trying to draw your next breath so you can keep running. When you are the runner yourself, it gets difficult in a hurry. But don't give up, whatever you do, even when the sweat runs into your eyes and you can hardly see, and even when you can't hear any cheers because your heart is beating so hard. Running without giving up may not sound too thrilling, but there's a real prize at the end if you don't disqualify yourself.

Keep serving, keep building yourself up in your faith, and keep on assuring yourself that it's worth it, because it is.

> Don't throw it all away now....It's still a sure thing! But you need to stick it out, staying with God's plan so you'll be there for the promised completion. It won't be long now, he's on the way; he'll show up most any minute. But anyone who is right

with me thrives on loyal trust; if he cuts and runs, I won't be very happy.

But we're not quitters who lose out. Oh, no! We'll stay with it and survive, trusting all the way.

—Hebrews 10:34–35, The Message

Read and reread Hebrews 10:34–35 when you are tempted to give up. That strong passage of Scripture is like a prescription for you when you are plagued with self-pity thoughts. ("I am so tired. I've waited so long already.") It helps you to get your confidence back. The New King James translation of verse 35 reads, "Therefore do not cast away your confidence, which has great reward." Rick Renner explains the richness of the meaning of this word in Greek:

> The word "confidence" is the Greek word *paressia*. This word means *boldness* and depicts a *very bold, frank, outspoken* kind of language. It carries the meaning of being *forthright, blunt, direct,* and *straight to the point.* In this verse, it refers to the *bold, brave, fearless* declarations and faith confessions regarding God's promises that these believers had been making.[4]

This brings us back to the idea of making strong, faith-building declarations to yourself. Do it when you're tired of running the race. Do it *before* you get tired. God is your strength. Keep on trusting Him, and you are not going to become disqualified in any way.

100 Percent Focus

Whether or not you are feeling disqualified in some way right now, your best protection against it is to be 100 percent focused on God, *not on what He has you doing.* The work itself will not give you the strength or the willpower to continue indefinitely. You will waver and wander and maybe even fall by the wayside.

You need to keep your relationship with God fresh and alive. Talk to Him about what you're doing and what you're thinking. Tell Him how you feel. Allow Him to talk to you and help you. He's more willing than you know to be your shepherd, every minute of every day. Yes, He will give you plenty of assignments, and you will need to work hard. But the assignments—even though they come from God—are not your goal. He is.

Oswald Chambers put this truth into words for us:

> Our Lord's primary obedience was to the will of His Father, not to the needs of people—the saving of people was the natural outcome of His obedience to the Father. If I am devoted solely to the cause of humanity, I will soon be exhausted and come to the point where my love will waver and stumble. But if I love Jesus Christ personally and passionately, I can serve humanity, even though people may treat me like a "doormat." The secret of a disciple's life is devotion to Jesus Christ, and the characteristic of that life is its seeming insignificance and its meekness. Yet it is like a grain of wheat that "falls into the ground and dies"—it will spring up and change the entire landscape (John 12:24).[5]

No, you are not disqualified, because of Jesus. His own words recap the advice:

Give your entire attention to what God is doing right now, and don't get worked up about what may or may not happen tomorrow. God will help you deal with whatever hard things come up when the time comes.

—Matthew 6:34, THE MESSAGE

Apart from me you can do nothing.

—John 15:5, NLT

CHAPTER 6

IMPARTING THE ANOINTING

I HAVE NEVER SEEN a generation like the one I am seeing today—a generation that is so hungry for more of God. I believe that *impartation* is the vehicle that God is using to satisfy this deep hunger. Read this chapter with expectation. I believe the Holy Spirit is going to release to you a passion for Him and for this generation, and that as a result of your passionate obedience, multitudes of people will be delivered and set free. Through the willingness of people like you, willingness to pay the price of this impartation and to release this anointing, we are going to see the greatest End-Time revival that we have ever experienced.

Webster's dictionary defines the word *impart* as "to give, or to bestow." The term translated "impart" in the New Testament comes from the Greek word *metadidomi*, which means "to give over" or "to share." Impartation from God allows the power of almighty God to flow through people like you and me. It is not confined to just a few or an elite group of people; God can and will use whatever vessel through whom He chooses to give, bestow, or share His blessings to another, just because He wants to. Paul knew this when he wrote to the Romans, "I long to visit you so that I can *impart* to you the faith that will help your church grow strong in the Lord" (Rom. 1:11, TLB, emphasis added). He was confident in his ability through

Christ to impart faith and strength, and he was also sure of God's willingness to pour into their lives through his obedience.

Jesus Christ is our greatest example. He is our master imparter, and He is the model that we must always follow. As we look through the Scriptures we will find many that refer to Jesus imparting to others. Luke 9:1 gives us Jesus's theology and His perspective about imparting the anointing: "Then He called His twelve disciples together and gave them power and authority over all demons, and to cure diseases." Notice this:

> All twelve disciples received power and authority, even Judas, not because of anything they had done, but because Jesus chose to give it to them. He imparted to them, drawing from the very power and authority he had within himself. He could do so because he wasn't lacking in either. Luke 9:2 tells us His purpose in imparting power and authority to His disciples. "He sent them out to preach the Kingdom of God and to heal the sick." In this verse, the word *preach* means, "to herald, to proclaim." Just like the disciples, we are called to be heralds. You must proclaim the Kingdom of God to everyone you meet. Each of us is a mouthpiece for the things of God. We are a part of His great market campaign. Not all of us will be pulpit preachers, but we are all commissioned and can be empowered to tell people about our Savior.[1]

I think that it is interesting that this is the first time that we see in the Bible the word *apostoles*, which means "one sent forth." The disciples have been set apart, empowered, and anointed to go and touch a broken world.

But this was just the beginning. Now Jesus wanted to expand the impartation of power and authority to a larger group—a group of seventy-two. Can you see the principle of multiplication here? Jesus is never satisfied with the stagnant or clique mentality ("us four and no more"). Instead, He uses impartation to expand the kingdom because impartation leads to multiplication.

Here, in the form of an equation, is how Jesus turned the twelve disciples into seventy-two:

1 (anointed Jesus)

x 12 (empowered apostles)

x 6 (people discipled by each apostle)

= 72 (disciples healing the sick, casting out demons, and winning the lost)

Scripture doesn't actually tell us whether the first twelve disciples helped disciple and empower the other sixty. Jesus could have and probably did personally impart into all of them, but it also would seem logical that He would use His closest disciples to model successful impartation.

Jesus began the ongoing process of reaching the world when He multiplied Himself through impartation into His followers. The number of people whose lives were transformed by God grew exponentially as Jesus and His followers continued to do this. But without impartation, that multiplication could not have been achieved.[2]

DON'T MISS YOUR MOMENT OF IMPARTATION

You really don't want to miss your moment if it is a moment of impartation. In a moment of impartation, God gives you exactly what you will need for what's ahead of you. You may not know what's ahead of you, and you may not realize yet what you'll need, but God knows.

In your moment of impartation, God *anoints* you so that you can operate in *His* supernatural strength instead of your own. You always need to receive an impartation of His power in order to do whatever He has called you to do. What it comes down to is that God calls us to do tasks that simply cannot be achieved in our own strength. Maybe you can fake it for a while, but you will not succeed if you try to perform supernatural work with your natural human strength. It's just too big for you. God's strength is so superior to yours.

> ANOINTING GIVES YOU ENERGY AND JOY, A SENSE OF TIMING AND STRATEGIES. SOMETIMES IT LEADS TO FINANCIAL PROVISION, POSSESSIONS, OR PROPERTY— WHATEVER YOU MAY NEED TO ACCOMPLISH GOD'S PURPOSES.

I'm not talking here only about raising the dead or healing the sick. I'm talking about *everything* God calls you to do. Has He called you to take care of your elderly mother-in-law? You need His anointing in order to do that with His love and wisdom and patience. Has He called you to go someplace to spread the good news? Don't leave home without His anointing. Has He called you to mentor and impart the anointing into young people's lives? You better be anointed (and have a lot of energy). The anointing is the power of God to serve Him and to serve others.

Even though it is so important to receive God's anointing before you do His work, you don't have to worry about getting hold of it. He already knows you need it, and it's His job to impart it to you. It's a gift, from Him to you. You are the receiver, and all you need to do is offer Him a receptive spirit. Openly receive whatever kind of anointing He wants to give you, because you can't dictate the terms of it.

When you receive His anointing (in other words, if you don't miss your moment of impartation), you will find that you can step up to a new dimension. You will have such a sweet fellowship with Him, and you will know immediately when He empowers you spiritually, mentally, and physically to battle anything that may come your way. You will be able to leave behind many of the things that used to be obstacles and hindrances to you. God will be with you in a new way, and you will know it. This is a precious gift He has given you, and you will be grateful for it.

After a while, God may begin to use you to impart the same kind of anointing in other people. That's often the way it works. You'll be glad to share it. You will want to bring others "on board" with you. It won't deplete your own anointing in the least. It's like your anointing includes a desire to impart itself to others.

What Is God's Anointing?

What am I talking about? What is God's anointing? Specifically, what kind or kinds of anointing should you be looking for?

First of all, you can't see an anointing except by its evidence. An anointing includes invisible elements, such as faith and vision and encouragement. An anointing gives you energy and joy. It gives you a sense of timing and strategies. Sometimes it leads to financial provision, possessions, or property—whatever you may need to accomplish God's purposes.

In order to have the anointing on your life you must be as the disciples were in Acts 4:13:

> Now when they say the boldness of Peter and John, and perceived that they were uneducated and untrained men, they marveled. *And they realized that they had been with Jesus.*
> —Acts 4:13, emphasis added

That is it in a nutshell—to be with Jesus over and over again. Not just for a few fleeting moments or when you need something, but to be with Him all the time. He is your very life and existence.

I'll tell you another thing: an anointing will *change* you. Immediately after he anointed Saul as king, the prophet Samuel said to him:

> You will meet a band of prophets coming down from the place of worship. They will be playing a harp, a tambourine, a flute, and a lyre, and they will be prophesying. At that time the Spirit of the LORD will come powerfully upon you, and you will prophesy with them. *You will be changed into a different person.*
> —1 Samuel 10:5–6, NLT, emphasis added

It happened just the way it had been prophesied. Saul met the prophets, and he was changed in a moment. He was changed from a man who couldn't even find his father's lost donkeys into a prophet of God who would also become the new king of Israel. His family and friends hardly recognized him as the same Saul they had known:

> As Saul turned and started to leave, God gave him a new heart, and all Samuel's signs were fulfilled that day. When Saul and his servant arrived at Gibeah, they saw a group of prophets coming toward them. Then the Spirit of God came powerfully upon Saul, and he, too, began to prophesy. When those who knew Saul heard about it, they exclaimed,

"What? Is even Saul a prophet? How did the son of Kish become a prophet?"

—1 Samuel 10:9–11, NLT

Saul was changed in a moment. The impartation of an anointing can happen in a moment, and so can the change that goes with it. If you miss your moment of impartation, you miss out on the changes too. Even if you feel that you're not ready (Saul did), God can do amazing things with you. That's always the point—you're miserably under-equipped to do what God wants you to do, so He equips you by anointing you and changing you.

The prophet Isaiah wrote about God's kind of changing work:

> …I, the LORD,
> am your Savior and your Redeemer,
> the Mighty One of Israel.
> I will exchange your bronze for gold,
> your iron for silver,
> your wood for bronze,
> and your stones for iron.
> I will make peace your leader
> and righteousness your ruler.
>
> —Isaiah 60:16–17, NLT

God always exchanges *upward*. You get His gold for your bronze. You get His strength for your weakness. You get exactly what you need in order to fulfill your destiny.

God's Anointing Oil

In the Bible, *anointing* means pouring oil onto a person or a thing to consecrate him or it for God's service and to impart His blessing and grace. The word is used a lot more in the Old Testament than it is in the New because it was such an important part of Jewish tradition and all of the cultural traditions of those times.

Anointings were especially significant for establishing a new king or leader. When Aaron was made into the head priest for the Israelites in the desert, God told Moses, "Then shalt thou take the anointing oil, and pour it upon his head, and anoint him" (Exod. 29:7, KJV).

Anointing was also used to refresh and restore, as we read in the familiar words of Psalm 23, verse 5: "Thou anointest my head with oil; my cup runneth over" (KJV).

Sometimes "anointing" includes something besides plain oil, as when the woman poured fragrant, perfumed oil over Jesus's head at Simon's house. By doing so, she was honoring Him in the most extravagant way possible, and her act resulted in Jesus honoring her in return:

> When Jesus was in Bethany at the house of Simon the leper, a woman came to Him having an alabaster flask of very costly fragrant oil, and she poured it on His head as He sat at the table. But when His disciples saw it, they were indignant, saying, "Why this waste? For this fragrant oil might have been sold for much and given to the poor."
>
> But when Jesus was aware of it, He said to them, "Why do you trouble the woman? For she has done a good work for Me. For you have the poor with you always, but Me you do not have always. For in pouring this fragrant oil on My body, she did it for My burial. Assuredly, I say to you, wherever this gospel is preached in the whole world, what this woman has done will also be told as a memorial to her."
>
> —Matthew 26:6–13

Besides all that, most of the time an anointing carries with it God's blessings and His authority and the grace to execute His will. Very often, it carries healing:

So the disciples went out, telling everyone they met to repent
of their sins and turn to God. And they cast out many demons
and healed many sick people, anointing them with olive oil.

—Mark 6:12–13, NLT

THE OIL OF THE SPIRIT

How does this idea of "anointing" apply to us today?

What we mean is the presence of the Holy Spirit Himself saturating us. God's Spirit fills our thinking and helps us follow the
Lord:

But the anointing which you have received from Him abides in
you, and you do not need that anyone teach you; but as the same
anointing teaches you concerning all things, and is true, and is
not a lie, and just as it has taught you, you will abide in Him.

—1 John 2:27

Often we mean the endorsement and empowering that comes
with His Spirit. The Amplified Bible translates Isaiah 61:1 this way:

The Spirit of the Lord God is upon me, because the Lord
has *anointed* and *qualified* me to preach the Gospel of good
tidings to the meek, the poor, and afflicted; He has sent me to
bind up and heal the brokenhearted, to proclaim liberty to the
[physical and spiritual] captives and the opening of the prison
and of the eyes to those who are bound.

—Isaiah 61:1, AMP, emphasis added

Under the anointing, along with being endorsed or qualified
to preach and teach with authority, our words convey miracle-
working power. The Holy Spirit quickens or fills with life the very
word of God, and it accomplishes that for which it is sent. "For the

word of God is living and powerful, and sharper than any two-edged sword" (Heb. 4:12).

> From the birth of Jesus to His resurrection, the Holy Spirit was anointing His words, ministry and every facet of His life. He was conceived by the Holy Spirit. As the Anointed One, His very presence in Mary's womb caused John the Baptist to be filled with the Spirit in Elizabeth's womb. As He was presented in the temple by His parents, Simeon gave glory to God that the anointed one, Christ, had finally come for the consolation of Israel. The anointing of the Holy Spirit on His life was so apparent that the scribes and teachers were amazed at His wisdom. On the day of His baptism, a dove, representing the Holy Spirit, came upon Him as evidence of His anointing. Within two months of His baptism, Jesus was boldly proclaiming His anointing in the temple (Luke 4). And we are promised that if the same Spirit who raised Christ from the dead dwells in us, He will quicken (bring to life) our mortal bodies as well.[3]

When Peter was preaching to Cornelius and his household, he talked about Jesus being anointed. He said:

> ...that word you know, which was proclaimed throughout all Judea, and began from Galilee after the baptism which John preached: how *God anointed Jesus of Nazareth with the Holy Spirit and with power,* who went about doing good and healing all who were oppressed by the devil, for God was with Him.
> —Acts 10:37–38, emphasis added

That's the same anointing that we know best—the anointing with the Holy Spirit and with power. It's intangible and invisible in a way, and yet Rod Parsley says that God's anointing is quite "tangible and transferable." He describes what he means:

> The anointing is a tangible force. Many people have difficulty understanding that truth, but I want you to comprehend the fullness of God's most precious anointing.
>
> It is not something God dangles in front of you like a carrot for a horse. It is completely within your grasp, and God wants you to have it.
>
> It is tangible, and it can be transferred. It was transferred from Elijah to Elisha through a mantle. It was transferred from Paul through handkerchiefs and aprons to those who were sick and afflicted.
>
> The anointing of God comes from the very throne of heaven. It comes full of power, full of energy to root up, to pull down, and to destroy every yoke of bondage the devil tries to put on you.[4]

Anointing with oil is another symbol of the Holy Spirit's anointing. There is a powerful release of His healing power when we follow the instructions of James. We often quote James 5:14: "Is any sick among you? let him call for the elders of the church; and let them pray over him, anointing him with oil in the name of the Lord" (KJV). Anointing with oil may be symbolic, but it is powerful when mixed with faith. But remember, the presence of the Holy Spirit's anointing on our life should be as tangible as the oil we can touch, see, and feel. But the kind of anointing I'm talking about in this chapter is the anointing *with the Holy Spirit and with power*.

MULTIPLYING THE BLESSING

My grandmother and mother imparted their anointing to me, and others have imparted still more. You may not have had godly parents, but God will bring people into your life who can impart God's power to you. He knows you need it, and it is part of God's equipping for your journey.

Sometimes, what we call an anointing is real basic—an anointing of strong *faith*. The apostle Paul mentored the young man Timothy, who had received an anointing of faith from his mother and grandmother. Paul urged Timothy not to forget what that faith could accomplish:

> I call to remembrance the *genuine faith* that is in you, which dwelt first in your grandmother Lois and your mother Eunice, and I am persuaded is in you also. Therefore I remind you to stir up the gift of God which is in you through the laying on of my hands.
>
> —2 Timothy 1:5–6, emphasis added

This anointing of faith was more important than being mentored by Paul himself. Such an anointing is an "impartable" thing, and it lives and grows within you. Even if you didn't have a godly mother or grandmother, you can receive such an anointing from God Himself. Most often, you will receive it through another believer (particularly from somebody who has some authority in your life).

WHEN YOU'RE ANOINTED, IT'S AS IF JESUS HIMSELF WALKS INTO THE ROOM. HIS SUPERNATURAL REALITY COMES IN WITH CLOTHES ON— *YOUR* CLOTHES.

You will find that not only are you anointed for a specific, limited task, but you can also be anointed for a lifetime calling. You can receive multiple anointings, and they can build on each other.

It's Supernatural

What does the anointing do? It releases your spiritual gifts and endows them with supernatural life—which is a great improvement on your natural life. Your *anointed* preaching is better in every way. It's not just loud; it gets heard by your listeners, and it delivers God's love and conviction straight to the hearts of those who hear you. Your *anointed* teaching is clearer and more insightful. People "get it," and their eyes light up. Your *anointed* singing brings the glory of the Lord into the room, and it changes people from passive listeners into passionate worshipers.

When you're anointed, it's as if Jesus Himself walks into the room. His supernatural reality comes in with clothes on—*your* clothes. Depending on the gifts He has given you and the circumstances in the room at that moment, He activates what are called "utterance gifts" such as prophecy, preaching, teaching, tongues, and interpretation. Or He activates the revelational "knowledge gifts" such as the word of knowledge, the word of wisdom, or the gift of discerning of spirits. It doesn't matter how you classify the gifts. Prophecy could be considered either type of gift. And I'm not saying that you have only one "anointable" gift in your possession or one gift at a time. Sometimes He activates several gifts in one person or in more than one person. Whatever He does in a given situation, it has to be Him doing it or there's not any anointing going on.

After Jesus died and was resurrected, He bestowed His Holy Spirit on believers so that we could represent Him throughout the earth. Today in the twenty-first century, that same powerful Holy Spirit who anointed Peter in the Book of Acts anoints you. How about that! It's supernatural, and it's real. You don't want to miss out on it. (If you haven't already experienced the infilling of the Holy Spirit, start seeking Him today.)

When I was a young girl, I started going places with my family to minister. Usually it went all right. The music was in tune, and the people were blessed. But I knew that I needed to be filled with the Spirit as my mom and sisters were. I needed to be baptized (which is like a superanointing) and anointed so that I could minister with more supernatural power.

> PRAY FOR GOD'S SUPERNATURAL ANOINTING OF BOLDNESS AND POWER. HE'LL RESPOND TO YOUR REQUEST.

When it happened, everybody around me knew it. I could not speak in English for three days straight. All I could do was speak and sing in my prayer language. I couldn't eat and I couldn't sleep. I remember drinking water and juice, but mostly I was overwhelmed with the power of God. You have to realize how unusual that is for a twelve-year-old to be engrossed in the power of God to that extent. It has to be a supernatural occurrence.

After that time, my life was never the same. I had been such a shy child. I had been so bashful that my parents used to have to bribe me to sing for just a few friends at home. When I was about five years old, even when I knew I'd get a whole dollar for singing one song, I would cry throughout the whole thing.

Then the boldness of God came upon me when I was baptized in the Holy Spirit. I still felt like I was the same Judy, but now I had the courage I needed to speak up for God. It was very much like it was in the Book of Acts when Jesus told the disciples, "You shall receive power when the Holy Spirit has come upon you" (Acts 1:8), and it came true. Those believers needed supernatural power in order to perform supernatural deeds, and they got it.

ANOINTED AND BOLD

It's going to be the same for you. There is a boldness that comes along with the Holy Spirit's power. He anoints people with a boldness that matches up with the call on their lives. It's not the same kind of boldness for each person, because each person's call is so different. I need boldness to get up on a stage and sing in front of thousands of people and television cameras, and my singing needs to bring people into God's presence. But the sister who goes out on the streets to minister to the homeless people has a different anointing. It's the same Holy Spirit who anoints us for our work, even though the calling and the work are very different from person to person.

Pray for God's supernatural anointing of boldness and power. He'll respond to your request. He promised to anoint you with power—you and your sons and daughters. I prayed for my two young daughters to receive God's anointing, and I've heard them speak in tongues. I've watched the power of God in them. I've heard them say things prophetically.

There was one time when Erica was really sick with bronchitis. She was three years old at the time. I'd been up in the night with her, and she'd been coughing and obviously having difficulty breathing. Our little family was lying in the bed with her, and we were just having our devotions. Jamie and I were just trying to get everyone settled. We began to pray for Erica. It wasn't the boisterous kind of prayer; it was just a nice, little, simple,

"Lord, touch Erica in her body. Bring healing, Father." All of a sudden something rose up in Kaylee, who was six. "Mom!" she said, "We've got to get up off this bed, and we've got to walk, and we've got to pray. And we've got to pray *loud*. And we've got to anoint Erica with oil. We've got to command the devil to get out of her." She went and grabbed a bottle of oil, and just before she proceeded to completely baptize her baby sister in olive oil, I grabbed it. We each put some oil on our fingers and, yes, we got off the bed and got violent in our faith and in our prayers. Kaylee prayed the hardest and the loudest. The next morning, Erica woke up completely free of bronchitis. Her lungs were completely clear, and she wasn't sick anymore.

The Holy Spirit had just come onto Kaylee, and we all knew it. She got anointed to pray for her sister's healing. All I did was follow along and say "Amen." I was not the one who was anointed for Erica's healing; it was her sister. It really shows the way God's anointing works *according to His will*. He wanted to heal Erica, and He wanted to use Kaylee. He filled her mind with the idea, and He gave her the boldness and the faith she needed.

Your anointings are like your spiritual gifts in that they are *given* to you. Although you can ask for them, you can't command them, and you certainly cannot manufacture them yourself. Nine times out of ten, you won't know quite how it happened. But you will know it came from God's Holy Spirit.

The Bible says, "The wicked flee when no one pursues, but the righteous are bold as a lion" (Prov. 28:1). In the early church, Peter and John and the other disciples were so bold that the Bible reports that the Pharisees and Sadducees could tell that they had "been with Jesus" (Acts 4:13). We are living in a day when the world needs to see and recognize that we have been with Jesus because of the miracles, signs, and wonders that follow us.

The disciples were getting unheard-of results. Hopeless cripples were getting healed. Sinners were being converted. This was such amazing evidence of the anointing of God that even the people who were not getting healed had to take notice. This boldness was even more remarkable because they could tell that these men were just ordinary guys. You and I are ordinary too. It's the anointing of God that makes all the difference.

> DON'T EVER THINK, EVEN FOR ONE MINUTE, THAT YOU CAN OBEY THE CALL OF GOD ON YOUR LIFE WITHOUT THE ANOINTING OF HIS SPIRIT.

The people knew that they had been with Jesus. In the same way, people are going to know that you have been with Jesus because of your boldness and authority.

THE IMPARTATION OF ANOINTING

Jesus had *imparted* His anointing to Peter and John and the other disciples. He did it directly. He still does that today sometimes because He can appear to whomever He wills. But usually He imparts an anointing to you through another anointed believer, somebody you respect. It's almost as if it "rubs off" on you. As Mike Murdock says, "The anointing you respect is the anointing that increases in your life."[5]

The last great thing that Jesus did was impart His anointing to His disciples. He put His blessing on them, and their whole lives were changed after that. Elijah did that too when he imparted his anointing to Elisha. My mother and her mother before her did the same thing for me. Have you received an anointing? Do you need another one? How can you position yourself so that you don't miss the anointing you need?

The most important thing you can do is get around people you respect, people whose anointing you would like to have rub off on you. That person may have to notice you first, as Elijah did Elisha, who was just plowing his father's field with his oxen. The Lord God had told Elijah to seek him out and to anoint him as prophet in his place (1 Kings 19:16). How did he anoint Elisha?

> Elijah went and found Elisha son of Shaphat plowing a field. There were twelve teams of oxen in the field, and Elisha was plowing with the twelfth team. Elijah went over to him and threw his cloak across his shoulders and then walked away. Elisha left the oxen standing there, ran after Elijah, and said to him, "First let me go and kiss my father and mother good-bye, and then I will go with you!"
>
> Elijah replied, "Go on back, but think about what I have done to you."
>
> So Elisha returned to his oxen and slaughtered them. He used the wood from the plow to build a fire to roast their flesh. He passed around the meat to the townspeople, and they all ate. Then he went with Elijah as his assistant.
>
> —1 Kings 19:19–21, NLT

Elijah, in obedience to the word of the Lord, had to find Elisha. But Elisha had to respond. Elijah anointed him by throwing his own mantle around Elisha's shoulders. But Elisha had to respond wholeheartedly. He slaughtered the oxen as an offering to God and also as a way to make a complete break with his past as a farmer who worked the soil. He slaughtered the oxen and burned up the yoke to show that he wouldn't be working the soil anymore. He got his old life out of the way so he could be changed into a prophet. Later, when Elijah was about to be transported into heaven, Elisha insisted on staying as close to his master as possible so that he would be able to receive a double portion of Elijah's anointing. His persistence paid off.

Don't Forget About It

Why am I talking so much about the anointing? Because I don't want you to leave home without it. I don't want you to get into trouble and not be able to figure out what happened. And I don't want you to ever think, even for one minute, that you can obey the call of God on your life without the anointing of His Spirit. You can't do it.

As I said in chapter 5, sometimes you just have to talk to yourself. You have to remind yourself what the truth is. You may even have to do it in front of a mirror. Stand there and address yourself: "It's just You and me, God, but You and me make a majority. God is for me, so who can be against me? I am called. I am appointed. I am *anointed*. So I'm going to make it. The Lord is on my side. He's faithful. He's true. He'll never let me down." Your voice represents your authority, and you're using it to convince yourself of the truth.

The truth is that you are the anointed of the Lord. Don't miss it!

Making It Happen

I just mentioned the idea of putting yourself around people who already carry the anointing you desire so that it will rub off on you.

I like to say it this way: "The anointing is usually caught, not taught." You usually don't get it from some university or some professor, although education is good. You get it usually because you possess such a hunger and thirst after God and His power that you will do almost anything to get it. Peter and John were around Jesus, and their boldness showed it. If you get around Benny Hinn, you will be healed—and you may be anointed to pray for others to be healed as well. Get around T. D. Jakes, and you will get anointed to get loosed. Get around Marilyn Hickey, and you will have an insatiable desire to know the Word by heart, and you will get anointed to memorize the Bible. Get around me, and you will get bold in your God, and God will use you in power and in authority because these are some of the gifts that I possess through the name of Jesus! You just find people you can click with, people who will sharpen you, people who will speak into your life. God has put all kinds of people together in the body of Christ. The only way we can all function together under His lordship is if we live and breathe in the Spirit at the same time.

> SEEK HIS KINGDOM AND HIS RIGHTEOUSNESS, AND THEN HOLD OUT YOUR OPEN HANDS FOR THE ANOINTING.

Another thing you can do to receive an anointing from God is ask and *seek*. Remember the "seek-add principle" I talked about in chapter 2? If you "seek first the kingdom of God and His righteousness, and all these things shall be added to you" (Matt. 6:33). Ask God to anoint you. Seek His anointing. He will not disappoint you. He wants you to have His anointing more than you want to have it.

What if you have been seeking but so far have not found anything? Oswald Chambers says it in just a few words: "Seek if you have not found."[6] He says the most likely reason you have not yet found what you are seeking is because of the principle in James 4:3—you may be "asking amiss." If you are asking out of your desire for self-fulfillment or because you want your life to be easier or you want to be "known" as this, that, or the other, don't be surprised if God doesn't anoint you with power for that. He's waiting for you to turn your heart around so that *He* is first. Seek His kingdom and His righteousness, and then hold out your open hands for the anointing.

While you're at it, remember to *be open* to whatever He sends. Sometimes His anointing comes in unusual packages. When Paul was shipwrecked on Malta (Acts 27–28), he was so anointed that he wasn't even hurt when a deadly viper bit his hand. I don't think he had expected events to work out the way they did. He just trusted God to keep him safe and to anoint him for every challenge, which He did.

Do you know one thing that really helps a lot? Getting rid of your junk. That's right. Not the junk in your kitchen junk drawer, but the junk in your heart and life. Take stock. What's in there? Are you all cluttered up with fleshly and worldly concerns? Are you more worried about getting your next appointment before some crowd so that you can show off your gift than you are about having a pure heart? Maybe that has something to do with your anointing, or the lack of it.

> Who may ascend into the hill of the Lord?
> Or who may stand in His holy place?

> He who has clean hands and a pure heart,
> Who has not lifted up his soul to an idol,
> Nor sworn deceitfully.
> He shall receive blessing from the LORD,
> And righteousness from the God of his salvation.
>
> —Psalm 24:3–5

If you're seeking the things of the world, you will be engrossed with the things of the world. If you're seeking the things of God, you will be engrossed with the things of God. That's the reason the Bible says you can't serve two masters, God and mammon. "Mammon" stands for worldly systems. It's not just money; it's the whole worldly system. If you live for God, everything you possess will be dedicated to Him. Your time, your money, your energy, your whole life will be His. But if you live for the world, your time, money, energy, and life will be going toward maintaining your little piece of the action.

In order not to ask amiss and in order not to miss your moment of anointing, you need to keep your heart fixed on God. Jesus said:

> Beware! Don't always be wishing for what you don't have. For real life and real living are not related to how rich we are....All mankind scratches for its daily bread, but your heavenly Father knows your needs. He will always give you all you need from day to day if you will make the Kingdom of God your primary concern.
>
> —Luke 12:15, 30–31, TLB

> Seek the LORD and His strength;
> Seek His face evermore!
>
> —Psalm 105:4

CHAPTER 7

GOD'S STRONG ANOINTED

I N OUR FAMILY of twelve, there were six of us Jacobs sisters who sang and one brother who played the bass guitar. We grew up singing and ministering together, and every one of us knew how important God's anointing was. Without Him, we were just another family singing group in our southern gospel heritage tradition, trying to make a name for ourselves. But with the strong anointing of God on our lives, it wasn't important whether or not we could sing or make a name for ourselves, because when He came and did His work through us and lives were changed, that's all that mattered.

All my life my family encouraged me by saying, "Judy, you can do anything through Christ Jesus who gives you strength. You are the anointed. You are the appointed. You get out there, girl. You get out there and sing under the anointing of God. And because it's *God's* anointing on you, be sure to cherish and protect it. If you walk a straight path and live in holiness and purity, God will keep His power and anointing on you, but if you stray away from Him, His anointing will leave." That's what I was told from the start. I was twelve when I started singing with my sisters, and I was almost scared even to drink a Coca-Cola lest God's anointing depart. That's the kind of culture I was raised in, and it made a permanent impression on me.

That may sound a little funny and a bit extreme, but it had good results. Because of it, I didn't grow up with some kind of low self-esteem problem. I never had to battle with my thoughts, wondering what people thought about me because I was a "woman speaker." I knew that I would stand before God one day for the anointing He had placed on my life and I would give an account to Him. So every time I stood on a stage, I gave God my very best, and He did the rest.

With that kind of encouragement from my family and the approach to ministry that they instilled in me, not only were we able to bless the people we ministered to, but also I grew up without any fear—except the fear of God. I really had almost no fear of man. I just grew up knowing that I didn't need to worry too much about what people said about me, because that's not what mattered. What mattered was what God said about me. I knew that He is the one who gives gifts, and He is the one who calls. He called me and anointed me to serve, so it went without saying that I had to go and do whatever God had called me to do, never mind what people might say. I learned that my audience was an audience of *One*. The only question was a simple one: was *He* happy when I finished?

> THE STRONG POWER OF ALMIGHTY GOD THAT GOT JESUS UP FROM THE GRAVE IS THE SAME POWER THAT IS GOING TO GET YOU UP AND GET YOU GOING IN YOUR DESTINY AND YOUR GOD-GIVEN PURPOSE.

That's why today I'm telling you the same thing my sisters told me. You are anointed. You are appointed. You can do anything through Christ Jesus who gives you the strength, and you can walk under a strong anointing on your life. Don't miss your moment. But watch your walk, because it matters.

BE AN ANOINTED ONE

I believe with all of my heart that there is a certain kind of anointing in the spirit realm that breaks heavy yokes. It breaks the back of sickness. It breaks diseases off people. When this kind of anointing is on you, it transforms situations and makes demons and devils go shrieking the other way.

This is the kind of anointing that was on Jesus. The Bible says plainly, "God *anointed* Jesus of Nazareth with the Holy Spirit and *with power*, who went about doing good and healing all who were oppressed by the devil, *for God was with Him*" (Acts 10:38, emphasis added). Now that tells me that if God was with Jesus on this earth, anointing Him with power and authority, then God's power is with us, helping us accomplish everything that He has called us to do. Paul said that the same power that raised Jesus from the dead would dwell in us. It was the strong power of almighty God that got Jesus up from the grave, and it is the same power that is going to get you up and get you going in your destiny and your God-given purpose.

In the Bible we read the story of a father bringing his son to Jesus and the disciples. His son was suffering from seizures; his demonic oppression often sent him leaping into fire and water. The man said that he had brought his son to be healed by Jesus's disciples, but "they could not cure him" (Matt. 17:16, KJV).

> Jesus rebuked the devil; and he departed out of him: and the child was cured from that very hour. Then came the disciples to Jesus apart, and said, Why could not we cast him out?…Howbeit this kind goeth not out but by prayer and fasting.
> —Matthew 17:18–19, 21, KJV

Sometimes in order to have what you have never had before, you must do what you have never done before. Sometimes you have to go after God with all that you have, and it will require some intense prayer and fasting.

Now, I hope you know that God's anointing isn't reserved only for a bunch of gospel singers and preachers and maybe a few kings in the Bible. No, He anoints parents and single people, steelworkers and office workers, men and women, young and old, single parents, single adults, employed and unemployed—anyone and everyone who responds to His call. But He never expects any of us to respond to His call in our own limited strength and with our own limited resources. You better believe that we need to be anointed with supernatural strength to respond to a supernatural call.

So when you think of "anointing," don't limit your idea of anointing to the preacher you watched on television last night or to your pastor or favorite worship leader. Maybe these people are anointed by God. Praise God if they are. But maybe they're not. Anointing isn't automatically furnished, even when you start preaching the gospel. Every preacher and singer has to ask God for His anointing and then accept it and take care of it when it comes.

It's the same for every other kind of anointing, including the one He wants to give you. Whatever God calls you to do, you can expect an anointing of His powerful Spirit to help you achieve it. What do you think God has called you to do? Are you doing it? Have you received His anointing for the assignment? You don't want to miss your moment of anointing just because you're paying more attention to *what* He's calling you to do than you are to *how* He expects you to do it. Or maybe you are so caught up into performance that you forget what all of this is about anyway.

Are you in school? Has He called you to be a student? Your customized anointing is going to equip you for studying, learning, and applying what you learn. God's Spirit will help you manage your time and energy while also giving you the ability to keep yourself pure in an environment that may not be that great. God will help you make good friends, and His Spirit in you will teach you how to bring His kingdom to your school or campus. You may be young, but God's anointing will provide wisdom for you so that you will know how to speak a word in season. Keep in touch with the Anointer by finding times to pray and people you can worship with.

> NO MATTER WHAT GOD HAS CALLED YOU TO DO, YOU CAN DO IT WITH CONFIDENCE BECAUSE HE WILL SUPPLY THE ANOINTING THAT YOU NEED FOR DOING IT.

Has God called you to be a mother of small children and hold down a job at the same time? Well, then, ask Him to anoint you with the right combination of gifts and grace so that you can hear Him in the midst of chaos, multitask without panic, and stretch your energy without snapping. You need His anointing so that you can possess an extra measure of peace, patience, and love.

Maybe you feel that God has called you to step out in faith and start a business or a ministry. Have you already gotten underway *without* the anointing He wanted to give you? It's not too late. Stop and ask this minute. For you, God's anointing will provide light for the next step of your venture so that you can walk with confidence and can say to Him, "Your word is a lamp to my feet and a light to my path" (Ps. 119:105). David said, "Commit everything you do to the LORD. Trust him, and he will help you" (Ps. 37:5, NLT).

God's anointing will open up your mind to creative ideas, lead you to well-timed connections, and release finances. He will provide you with extra energy, common sense, and a strong persevering spirit. He will make it possible for you to follow the advice in Ecclesiastes: "Whatever your hand finds to do, do it with your might" (Eccles. 9:10). You'll be doing it with all your might because God has laid His hands on yours.

Are you getting this? No matter what God has called you to do, you can do it with confidence because He will supply the anointing that you need for doing it. Don't miss your moment. It's right in front of you, if you have eyes to see it.

Jesus told His disciples, "But you shall receive power when the Holy Spirit has come upon you; and you shall be witnesses to Me in Jerusalem, and in all Judea and Samaria, and to the end of the earth" (Acts 1:8). The "end of the earth" includes your neighborhood, your workplace, and your favorite seat on the bus that you ride into the city on Thursdays. You shall receive an anointing of power to do whatever He calls you to do in whatever your corner of the earth happens to be. Regardless of what God's call is on your life, you can be sure that He wants you to be one of His anointed ones.

This psalm communicates a great deal of this:

> What joy for those whose strength comes from the LORD....
> They will continue to grow stronger,
> > and each of them will appear before God in
> Jerusalem.
> O LORD God of Heaven's Armies, hear my prayer.
> > Listen, O God of Jacob.
> O God, look with favor upon the king, our shield!
> > Show favor to the one you have anointed.
> A single day in your courts
> > is better than a thousand anywhere else!
> I would rather be a gatekeeper in the house of my God
> > than live the good life in the homes of the wicked.
> For the LORD God is our sun and our shield.
> > He gives us grace and glory.
> The LORD will withhold no good thing
> > from those who do what is right.
>
> —Psalm 84:5, 7–11, NLT

HALLMARKS OF ANOINTING

People who have not missed their God moments are the anointed ones, and they have certain things in common:

1. They have a knowledge of who Jesus is. He is a very real person in their lives. They know Him as their own God, not their mama's God, or auntie's God, but their God.

2. They have a working knowledge and understanding of the Word of God. It has become their very existence. So when the enemy comes, they hit him with

an "it is written." Anointed people are able to touch a hurting world with the words of their Lord.

3. They are always open to personal revelation that the Holy Spirit will impart into their lives through His Word, through another anointed vessel, or through prayer and fasting.

4. They are always open and ready for persecution. At the same time, a person who has an anointing will also carry a "glory" that will be visible. The Bible says, "All that will live godly in Christ Jesus shall suffer persecution" (2 Tim. 3:12, KJV). But if they bear it, then the Spirit of glory rests upon them. (See 1 Peter 4:14.)

5. They give themselves totally to God. Their spirits are open to hear and obey the voice of the Father. So when He says, "Fast three days," they fast three days. They belong to God—body, mind, soul, and spirit.

6. They can walk with boldness and authority, yet with gentleness and humility. They are able to see where God is working so they can work alongside Him. Their spiritual DNA has been changed, and that makes them able to grow in their ability to reflect the character of Jesus. They are more righteous all the time, and their path shines more and more all the time too, like the dawn: "The way of the righteous

is like the first gleam of dawn, which shines ever
brighter until the full light of day" (Prov. 4:18, NLT).

Where you are concerned, I know your call may be a hidden
one, but I also know that your role is an important one in the
kingdom of God. Many (maybe most) anointings are hidden
ones, but that does not diminish their importance. You *are* an
anointed one, and it's important that you operate in a full knowledge of that fact. You receive your anointing by faith, and you
walk in your anointing by faith.

Do you understand what I mean? What should a "walk" that is
anointed look like? Here are some of the most important character-
istics of what anointed walking in the Spirit looks like:

**You replace what "comes naturally" with something that comes
supernaturally.**

It is natural for you to walk naturally, according to your flesh.
No problem. Walking naturally is the same as walking by your
own strength only. When people who do what "comes naturally"
get up in the morning, it doesn't really matter which side of the
bed they get out on, so to speak. If they get out on the "wrong"
side, they just excuse their grumpiness because, you know, "It's
just the way I am sometimes."

However, when you "put on Jesus Christ," you have chosen to
"make no provision for the flesh" anymore (Rom. 13:14). You have
chosen to walk in a different way, and the more you do that, the
more you reflect the character of your Lord Jesus. You lean hard on
Him, and He helps you know what to do and how to do it. Paul told
the church in Galatia how this works: "Walk and live [habitually]
in the [Holy] Spirit [responsive to and controlled and guided by the

Spirit]; then you will certainly not gratify the cravings and desires of the flesh (of human nature without God)" (Gal. 5:16, AMP).

This goes along with what I said earlier, because you guard your anointing by watching your walk. If you try to do God's work in your own strength, you are destined to fail. Your own strength will never be sufficient for God's work. And if your anointing is not balanced with godly character, your anointing won't last.

With God's supernatural empowering, you will keep growing and changing. More and more, you will actually become the person you have always wanted to be—resilient and strong and confident and grateful and joyful and wise. You will be amazed at the things that will happen both inside you and outside you. You never thought you would see such powerful things. Sometimes it's the internal changes that are the most amazing. People will begin to see Jesus in you. You will be able to stay calm in a crisis. You won't fly off the handle anymore. Your conscience will become sensitive to the slightest stumble in your daily walk. Your thinking and decision making will be clearer and better. You will be able to love the unlovable and tolerate the intolerable. Whatever you need to be and do, God will provide for you. A person who has God's anointing is able to grow in all these wonderful ways, and that's what His anointing looks like.

> NO MATTER WHAT KIND OF PERSONALITY YOU HAVE, YOU CAN WALK IN BOLDNESS AND AUTHORITY TO DO THE THINGS GOD HAS SET BEFORE YOU.

You will walk in the abundant life.

As you walk with the Lord's anointing, "abundance" will become your middle name. You may not be wealthy, but you will rejoice in God's complete provision for you. You may have to walk through various trials—in fact, for sure you will, because God chastens those He loves (Prov. 3:11; Heb. 12:6; Rev. 3:19). But in spite of every hardship, you will have joy and peace deep down in your heart, as I already mentioned, and you will not be easily rattled.

Never again will you dread the days ahead. You'll never feel as if you're missing your full potential, because you'll be so sure that God is bringing you into your destiny. With God's anointing, your spirit will never grow old and shriveled up. Like a beautiful tree, you'll keep growing until the day you die, bearing fruit and enjoying giving it away.

You will exemplify God's grace in action.

In his first letter to the church, Peter wrote mostly about what "grace in action" looks like. At the end of the letter, he wrote, "This is the true grace of God in which you stand" (1 Pet. 5:12). What is grace composed of? If you're walking in God's anointing, you will be walking in God's grace, and you can expect to see more and more of the following "grace-full" qualities:

- Peace
- Joy
- Hope
- Love
- Faith
- Freedom from anxiety
- Protection from harm

- Sanctification, righteousness
- Endurance
- Ability to resist sin and the devil
- Humility
- Ability to do good works
- Ability to proclaim the gospel message
- Prayerfulness
- Sensitivity to God's Spirit
- Strength and energy

I have listed these in no particular order, because it's impossible to rank them by importance. They're all equally important, and they're all equally possible, all because of God's anointing on your life.

You will be bolder than you thought you were.

One unmistakable hallmark of God's anointing is boldness. Even people who are naturally shy become bolder when the Spirit comes. No matter what kind of personality you have, you can walk in boldness and authority to do the things God has set before you. Partnering with the Holy Spirit, you will step into divine appointments, and I'm sure you don't want to miss your moments for those. You may not be the one chosen to "close the deal" and bring somebody into new birth in Christ, but you will have assignments. And God will send you everything you need to complete the things He calls you to do.

Just recall what He did for Deborah. (Read the whole story in the Book of Judges, chapters 4–5.) She occupied an unusual position for the time—she was a judge in Israel, and she was a woman—and she seems to have carried more of the Lord's anointing than her male peers did. Barak, who commanded ten thousand strong warring men, respected Deborah so much that he didn't dare go into battle against the Canaanite army without her. This was an unusual thing indeed. Male pride alone could have caused him to decide to go it alone. After all, he was a seasoned commander, and his men were experienced and strong warriors. What did Deborah know about running a war?

But Barak knew about the power of anointing, and he could see who had the anointing for this situation; Deborah did. So he humbled himself and asked her to accompany him into the fight. Barak's humility paid off royally; the battle on the plain of Jezreel turned in his favor, and even the dreaded Canaanite commander, Sisera, was killed (by another woman, Jael). You can read about it in chapters 4–5 of the Book of Judges. Barak didn't get the credit, but his side did win the battle decisively, thanks to God's anointed and appointed judge Deborah.

Your personal God assignment may not be recorded for history, and it may not be quite as thrilling as Deborah's was, but your role is vital just the same. Let your life walk demonstrate your transformed life. Let the supernatural strength of the Lord show through everything you do.

You will pray unstoppable prayers.

Another unmistakable sign of God's anointing is a strong prayer life. You will pray as boldly as you speak and act, maybe even more boldly. Here's a good example of what I'm talking about, from the experience of Francis Frangipane:

> Prayer is stronger than kings and mightier than armies. Prayer is the most powerful force on earth.

I remember when my dad surrendered his life to the Lord. For ten years during our annual visits we clashed intellectually about God. Then one day he came "armed" with an argument many use against God. He said, "If there really is a God, why doesn't He always answer prayer?"

He was secure in his position and I was tired of the argument. I went into the bathroom and prayed, "Lord, You've got to give me an answer."

When I returned I could see that Dad felt he had won this round. I love my dad very, very much, so this is what I said: "Dad, forget all the people that you think didn't get answers to prayer—you yourself are an answer to prayer! You are alive today because our entire family daily prays for you." Then I continued, "But let's experiment. You say God doesn't answer prayer; we say He does. So for one week we won't pray for you, and we'll see what happens."

I cannot remember ever seeing my dad turn so pale. He looked over at Mom and said, "Hon, tell the boy not to do that." Then, with beads of sweat forming on his forehead, he said to me, "Okay. What do I have to do to keep you praying for me?"

In three minutes he went from disbelief in prayer to begging us to keep praying for him. I said, "Dad, the only way I'll keep praying for you is if you pray right now and give your life to Christ." The Lord answered my prayer.[1]

The Lord answered Francis Frangipane's prayer for his father, and He will answer your prayers as well. The bolder the prayers, the better, if you're attuned to the voice of God.

God loves to be asked. He loves to hear your voice. He loves it when you acknowledge that He is the source of every good thing and then ask Him for something. His anointing makes it possible for you to pursue Him in prayer. He gives you the perseverance you need to keep praying until you see the results. He sustains your faith, and He increases it.

The first requirement for powerful prayer is an unshakeable conviction that you have been invited to sit alongside of God's mercy seat in heavenly places. You—little ol' you—have "clout." You have the name of Jesus, the name above all names, and you have the Holy Spirit inside you, making sure that you pray what the Father wants you to pray. "But God, who is rich in mercy, for his great love wherewith he loved us, even when we were dead in sins, hath quickened us together with Christ, (by grace ye are saved;) and hath raised us up together, and made us sit together in heavenly places in Christ Jesus" (Eph. 2:4–6, kjv). *That's* being anointed!

Your life will witness louder than words.

So often it's true—your life can witness even louder than words. A friend's husband worked at one time for a company, and there was a man in his department who was one of those hard-to-get-along-with people—always complaining and making life difficult. One day, my friend's husband just reached the limit of his endurance, and he got angry. He said some strong words. A little later, he regretted it. So he went back to his co-worker and apologized for losing his temper—even though the man himself had done a lot more things wrong than simply losing his temper, even that same day. A few weeks later, one of the secretaries in the office asked my friend's husband a question. "Hey, did you come from somewhere else? You didn't grow up around here, did you?"

"Why do you ask? I grew up right in this area."

"Well, you act different. Like the other day when you apologized to Joe. I never saw anybody do something like that before. Most guys wouldn't have done that."

You and I know what was different about him. It wasn't because he grew up in a different part of the country where people grow up learning to be humble and asking forgiveness. Actually, he *was* from a different part of the country—heaven. His heavenly citizenship was showing. The Holy Spirit had made him different, and it showed. God's anointing oil was shining on his forehead.

THIS IS YOUR SEASON

Besides anointing you to stand strong for Him in a daily way, God has ordained special times and special seasons of anointing for your life. This is true for you, no matter what kind of person you are. You are entering into a new season of anointing right now; I am sure of it. Even the fact that you are reading about entering a season of anointing means you better get ready for one!

> SOMETIMES GOD MATCHES THE ANOINTING TO SOMEBODY'S PERSONALITY, AND SOMETIMES HE CHANGES THE PERSON TO MATCH THE ANOINTING.

Your season of anointing is going to involve a pulpit, because it involves opening your mouth in some way. But don't worry if you don't like public speaking. Your pulpit doesn't have to be in a church or at a worship event. You don't have to stand up in front of thousands of people with bright lights shining on you. Your pulpit may be in a prison or in a Sunday school class, or even at your kitchen sink. Whatever God has called you to do, He has anointed you to do it. You are called, and you are appointed to some kind of ministry, and you are anointed for it. Let me remind you once again: without the anointing, you have no business doing what God has called you to do.

The prophet Joel, speaking for God, said, "I will pour out My Spirit on all flesh; your sons and your daughters shall prophesy..." (Joel 2:28). That means you. *You* are anointed to prophesy. Prophecy means more than predicting the future; it also means preaching and proclaiming the Word of the Lord. You can do that just about anywhere. Wherever you open your mouth, you declare who God is. You—[put your name in here]—are one of the "sons and daughters" that Joel was talking about. Therefore, God's Spirit has been poured out on you, and you are anointed.

When Samuel came to select and anoint one of Jesse's sons to become the new king, God gave young David favor in Samuel's sight. That's because he had favor in God's sight. In your life, you can look for the same signs. Where do you have favor? God's anointing is just around the corner. Do you want it?

Things that have been holding you down and holding you back are getting ready to be loosed. Valleys are getting ready to be exalted. Mountains are getting ready to fall down. Crooked paths are getting straightened out. Rough places are about to be made smooth. Light is about to dawn in the darkness, and clarity is starting to come *if* you hold out your hands and let God's anointing equip you for the season He is bringing you into. All you need to do is agree with Him. Say yes, and hold out your hands. Get ready for a season of release and a season of increase.

Don't ever forget that you need God's anointing to do God's work. You cannot do it alone. Before you take another step, you'd better have His power. You'd better have His authority and His

Word. You'd better have that extra measure of faith that makes you able to lay hands on the sick, and they *will* recover.

As I said earlier, there is a yoke-destroying anointing that breaks the back and neck of sickness and disease. When this anointing is upon you, it will cause hopeless situations to change. This was the kind of anointing that was on Elisha when he prophesied to the king's assistant in the midst of the siege and famine that by the next day at that time, food would be abundant (2 Kings 6–7). There was a yoke-destroying anointing on Moses when he led the people of Israel out of bondage in Egypt. God likes to give people yoke-destroying anointings because He always wants to set people free. Have you fasted and prayed for something lately? The result of your fast may be a yoke-destroying anointing. God says:

> Is this not the fast that I have chosen:
> To loose the bonds of wickedness,
> To undo the heavy burdens,
> To let the oppressed go free,
> And that you break every yoke?
>
> —Isaiah 58:6

OPERATE IN THE ANOINTING GOD GIVES YOU

OK, I think I've made it pretty plain—God puts all kinds of anointings on people. God is very generous with His anointing oil. Sometimes He matches the anointing to somebody's personality, and sometimes He changes the person to match the anointing, as He did with Saul (1 Sam. 10). He gives long-term anointings, and He gives short-term anointings.

However He does it, His anointing becomes part of your DNA. It establishes you as a distinct individual, as His own child. It makes you look more like Him and act more like Him. It makes you able to operate in the gifts He has given you.

Most of you don't get to see me when I'm at home with my family, so you don't see me using my wife and mommy anointing very much, but when you see me up on a stage somewhere, you see me operating in my anointing to proclaim His Word. And you see me do it in a certain way that is unique to me. That's how God anointed me. If I came out in a flowery dress and tried to sing real soothing and pretty, you probably wouldn't recognize me. And if I stood still and straight behind the pulpit with my pile of typed notes in front of me and my glasses on my nose and spoke in a quiet voice into the microphone on its nice pulpit stand ("The flowers are beautiful. God is good. Springtime is coming. Everything is great. God bless you all…"), you really wouldn't recognize me. You'd get up and get out of there in a hurry. You'd be saying, "What's wrong with that girl? Something is wrong." You would be able to tell in an instant that I wasn't operating in my anointing. I don't think I could even fake it for a minute. I have to stay true to my divinely anointed DNA, and so do you.

> YOUR PURIFIED HEART, YOUR TRUSTING SPIRIT, AND YOUR FERVENT WORSHIP WILL BRING GOD'S ANOINTING QUICKLY.

Stay true to your anointing. Also, don't forget where you've come from (the better to praise God for bringing you out of it). Even more importantly, don't forget where you're going. You cannot live a victorious Christian life without the power of the Holy Spirit in you. You cannot live and do what God has called you to do or be who God has called you to be unless the boldness and authority of God have risen up in you in response to the anointing of His Spirit.

Are you feeling weak these days? Are you not so sure I'm telling the right person all about anointings? Well, please put this book down and look up to heaven. Stand up and look up. Hold out your hands. Let God's spotlight shine into your heart. Toss out everything you can think of that might be blocking God's anointing. And when your heart is as clean as your hands, receive the fresh anointing that God wants to give you. Open your mouth and praise Him. Lift your hands to heaven along with your smiling face. You will see what I mean when I say that your anointing will intensify. God has a real big bottle of anointing oil, and it never goes dry. Your purified heart, your trusting spirit, and your fervent worship will bring His anointing quickly.

In the Bible, we read about Hannah and Samuel. Hannah had been barren, as you know, and then God opened her womb as a result of her fervent prayer. Because of her anointing of faith, barren Hannah became pregnant, and her child, Samuel, grew up to become one of the most anointed prophet priests of Israel.

Here's what Hannah said when she brought her young son Samuel to dedicate him to the Lord's service. She praised God with her whole heart, and she told whoever would listen about the strength that comes with God's anointing:

> My heart rejoices in the Lord!
>   The Lord has made me strong.
> Now I have an answer for my enemies;
>   I rejoice because you rescued me.
> No one is holy like the Lord!

There is no one besides you;
    there is no Rock like our God....
The bow of the mighty is now broken,
    and those who stumbled are now strong.
Those who were well fed are now starving,
    and those who were starving are now full.
The childless woman now has seven children,
    and the woman with many children wastes away....
He will protect his faithful ones,
    but the wicked will disappear in darkness.
No one will succeed by strength alone.
    Those who fight against the Lord will be shattered.
He thunders against them from heaven;
    the Lord judges throughout the earth.
He gives power to his king;
    he increases the strength of his anointed one.
        —1 Samuel 2:1–2, 4–5, 9–10, NLT, emphasis added

CHAPTER 8

MADE TO MENTOR

I WANT TO WORK *with dead people.*

I didn't put that down for the shock value; I really mean it. When I say I want to work with dead people, I mean I want to work with people who have died to themselves or who are in the process of dying to themselves. I want to work with people who are dead enough to be turning the corner and coming alive in Christ. The best kind of people to work with are the people who are moving forward and changing into His likeness.

I want my life to count. That's why I want to work with people and minister to people and just be around people who are doing things God's way. My life on this earth is not going to be long enough to mess around with doing it my way. I want to participate in what God is doing and be an effective worker in His kingdom. As I do what God has called me to do in the body of Christ, of course I prefer it when I can see results.

Some of the best results of my preaching and teaching and one-on-one times happen with the people who are the "deadest." Truth is, my best efforts come when I'm at my deadest and weakest (2 Cor. 12:10). The "deader" I am to my old selfish ways, the faster I grow into the likeness of my Savior.

It's always true: the *only* way a person can change to become more like Jesus is if that person dies to his or her old self. Paul set the standard in his letter to the Romans as he made it clear how our own death to self is connected with Jesus's coming and suffering and death on the cross. In that letter, he said this:

> Therefore, dear brothers and sisters, you have no obligation to do what your sinful nature urges you to do. For if you live by its dictates, you will die. But if through the power of the Spirit you put to death the deeds of your sinful nature, you will live.
>
> —Romans 8:12–13, NLT

Our whole Christian life is one of putting our sinful nature to death and becoming more and more alive in Christ Jesus. That means we're all supposed to be dead people—or, more accurately, *resurrected* people. It's simple. You can't get resurrected if you don't die first. Death is your route to life.

> THE RESURRECTION LIFE GOES 'ROUND AND 'ROUND. IT'S A BIG OL' LIFE-GIVING CIRCLE.

This can be hard to keep in mind. To accomplish this, we really and truly need the rest of the members of the body of Christ. We can't stay on track if we try to go it alone. We need encouragement, love, and advice from our fellow "dead people." The New Testament is full of statements like these:

> Let the word of Christ dwell in you richly in all wisdom, teaching and admonishing one another in psalms and hymns and spiritual songs, singing with grace in your hearts to the Lord.
>
> —Colossians 3:16

Now I myself am confident concerning you, my brethren, that you also are full of goodness, filled with all knowledge, able also to admonish one another.

—Romans 15:14

So encourage each other and build each other up, just as you are already doing.

—1 Thessalonians 5:11, NLT

One of the greatest ways for all of us dead people to speed up the process of entering into Jesus's life is to have an active relationship with someone else who is more mature in Him—a mentor. Mentors have walked ahead of you on this pathway. They have more experience than you do in this dying-to-self thing. They also have a wealth of experience in successfully living the abundant life we talk about.

Have you had mentors in your walk with God? Do you have a mentor or two right now? Perhaps you have also now come to the stage in your life when you can mentor others. I don't want you to miss your moment to be mentored—or to mentor someone else. A mentor can make it possible for the breath of God to bring someone's spirit alive. (See Job 32:7–8.) Once someone's spirit starts to revive and come alive again with resurrection life, it is very likely that that person will also want to give God's life away, and they will become mentors too. The resurrection life goes 'round and 'round. It's a big ol' life-giving circle.

This chapter is about the process of taking in someone else's godly wisdom and sharing the wisdom you've gained. I think that mentoring is one of the all-around best ways to make sure you don't miss your moment to be resurrected in some part of your life.

Do You Want It?

When I was growing up, I had no mentors to help get me ready for what I'm doing today. I was already aware that I had a call on my life, but I didn't see any women preachers out there. Or if they were out there, I didn't hear about them. I just didn't see very many strong women of God except my own mother and sisters, and naturally their example was limited.

You can get wisdom in two ways: through a mentor or through mistakes. I've been the mistake route. I have all the T-shirts. It's not fun to learn everything the hard way.

It's also not a very good use of your time to learn everything the hard way when you can learn the same things more quickly and

> IT REQUIRES PERSISTENCE TO BE MENTORED. YOU CAN'T JUST DECIDE TO SAY GOOD-BYE AND START TO SHOP FOR A NEW PERSON TO MENTOR YOU.

with less pain through someone else's experiences. I don't want other women who are called to ministry to have to learn everything the hard way, as I did. So a few years ago, one of the things I decided to do was establish a place and an environment where women, and later on men too, could be mentored in a life of ministry.

My husband, Jamie, and I started the International Institute of Mentoring, and we offer meetings where we pull together a team of strong men and women who have a lot to offer leaders. As a team, we impart into powerful men and women of God who attend the institute, instruct them, and feed them the truth. They can ask questions and get answers.

They also get to know each other and develop a broader network of supportive relationships.

Some of what we do at the institute is spiritual mentoring—as a team, we make it our goal to come alongside each attendee with God's love. We serve the deep needs of their spirits. We talk about scriptural truth. As Jesus did with His disciples, we kneel down with towels and water and we wash their feet, which gives each woman a spiritual cleansing such as they may never have had before.

Some of what we do is purely practical mentoring—we talk about things like how a woman can make sure that her husband and children are properly cared for when she is on the road ministering or vice versa. We talk about being single. We talk about finances, taking care of our temple by putting the right foods into it. We also laugh a lot, and we pray and worship together. At our institute, the mentoring is packaged to fit a period of several days. Yet in that short time, true mentoring has only begun.

WHAT ARE YOU LOOKING FOR?

In our explanation of what a mentor is, we make sure that people also know what a mentor is not.

First, a godly mentor is filled with the Holy Spirit. The Spirit gives life to him or her, and that makes it possible for real life to be reproduced in you. From that point of view, it doesn't matter if your mentor is older than you are or younger. The words of young Elihu to Job are true: "Those who are older are said to be wiser, but it is not mere age that makes men wise. Rather, it is the spirit in a man, the breath of the Almighty that makes him intelligent" (Job 32:7–9, TLB). Another way you can tell a person might be a good mentor is that the person has common sense. Proverbs 16:21 says, "The wise man is known by his common sense" (TLB). So a mentor is filled with the Holy Spirit, a mentor is someone who is wiser than you are, and a mentor possesses down-to-earth common sense. Also:

- A mentor is a coach, a teacher, a guide, and a trusted counselor.
- A mentor is not a perfect person.
- A mentor is one whose advice you follow.
- A mentor loves you too much to leave you as you are.
- A mentor sees your enemy before you do.
- A mentor possesses persistence.

I might add that it requires persistence to *be* mentored as well. When you are a "mentee" (which is the word I use for a person who is being mentored), you need to stick with your mentor. If things get a little difficult, you can't just decide to say good-bye and start to shop around for a new person to mentor you. Figure out how you want your relationship to work, and stick with it so that both of you can benefit from it.

> A MENTOR GIVES GOD'S LOVE AWAY AND KEEPS THE FLOW GOING LONG ENOUGH FOR THE OTHER PERSON TO BEGIN TO DO THE SAME THING.

If you're going to find a mentor (or more than one—sometimes you have mentors for different aspects of your life), you have to *want* mentoring. Mentoring doesn't just happen. It is a process of seeking. First, you have to find a mentor, and that can take a while. You have to seek until you find the right person. After you find someone to mentor you, your seeking is not finished. Now the mentoring relationship itself requires you to seek more and more impartation. You have to stick with the relationship as you seek to learn everything your mentor can teach you.

LOVE IS THE KEY TO A MENTOR'S HEART

Mentoring is a little like parenting, which makes sense, because, after all, parents are the ultimate mentors to their children. If you are looking for a mentor, what does that mean to you? One thing it means is that you are looking for good "parent material."

Ask yourself, what kind of person is a good parent? Obviously, almost any adult man or woman can produce (or adopt) a child. But to become a truly good father or mother to that child, what does it take? It takes a long-term commitment to provide for that child for a very long time. Good parents must love and nurture their children. They must protect and provide for them. It's a big job, and the outcome is extremely important.

A good parent pays attention to the child's development and also to any detrimental influences. For example, good parents know that the media cannot be trusted to take good care of their child's mind and heart. Good parents know enough about what's out there to know that the typical teenager spends hours a day online, and today's teens are growing up as the first generation to have "point-and-click" pornography available to them. Good parents are not blind to the fact that almost 50 percent of the top-selling music CDs contain sexual content, and they know that if their child watches the average fifteen to seventeen hours of TV each week, he or she inevitably will see about fourteen thousand sexual scenes and references each year as well as an inordinate number of product advertisements that are broadcast without regard to the moral decay of young people. In other words, good parents realize that they need to protect their children, because the community and the world at large are certainly not going to do it.

However, good parents will not take the easy way out and simply forbid all contact with the world and isolate their children from everything. In fact, that's what *bad* parents might do. Instead, good parents will take advantage of "teachable moments" to help their children learn how to negotiate the dangers of life. Good parents know that the most loving thing they can do is equip their children to become capable, discerning, and mature adults.

Much like parents, mentors have loving hearts toward their mentees. Love is the key to a mentor's heart. I'm talking about God's kind of love. The Bible says that His kind of love protects and patiently endures:

> Love is patient and kind. Love is not jealous or boastful or proud or rude. It does not demand its own way. It is not irritable, and it keeps no record of being wronged. It does not rejoice about injustice but rejoices whenever the truth wins out. Love never gives up, never loses faith, is always hopeful, and endures through every circumstance.
> —1 Corinthians 13:4–7, NLT

Within real-life circumstances, mentors can love new life into people. When you have a mentor, you can keep reaching up and letting your mentor love life into you, and he or she will fill you up with God's love and provision. After a while, you will possess enough love and wisdom to reach out and love new life into someone else. That's how it works. A mentor gives God's love away and keeps the flow going long enough for the other person to begin to do the same thing.

Your mentor isn't necessarily going to be your local pastor or Bible teacher, but she (if you are female) will be someone who is like a mother, or he (if you are male) in a very real way will be like a good father. Look at what Paul wrote to the Corinthians:

> After all, though you should have ten thousand teachers (guides to direct you) in Christ, yet you do not have many fathers. For I became your father in Christ Jesus through the glad tidings (the Gospel).
>
> —1 Corinthians 4:15, AMP

Whether or not your mentor actually "begot" you when you were born again, you need to find someone with the heart of a father or mother who will help you grow up in Jesus.

PASSING ON THE KEYS OF THE KINGDOM

As I mentioned above, a mentor keeps the flow going. Another way of looking at it is to say that a good mentor passes on the keys of the kingdom of God. The keys of the kingdom unlock the riches of heaven. A good mentor will be able to show you how to live your life in agreement with God, as well as how to eliminate the things from your life that are not from God. Jesus said:

> I will give you the keys of the kingdom of heaven; and whatever you bind (declare to be improper and unlawful) on earth must be what is already bound in heaven; and whatever you loose (declare lawful) on earth must be what is already loosed in heaven.
>
> —Matthew 16:19, AMP

You don't want your life to be pointless, but that's what it will be if you don't get your hands on the keys of the kingdom and if you don't pass them on. The Book of Proverbs talks about this (I am quoting from two different versions):

> It is possible to give away and become richer! It is also possible to hold on too tightly and lose everything. Yes, the liberal man shall be rich! By watering others, he waters himself.
> —Proverbs 11:24–25, TLB

> The liberal person shall be enriched, and he who waters shall himself be watered.
> —Proverbs 11:25, AMP

You will be rich in the things that count if you give away the wisdom and love you have received.

One more thing: you are never too old to keep on being mentored. No matter what your age is, keep seeking out mentoring, even if sometimes you have to resort to old books and distant preachers to fill in as your mentors.

Needless to say, you're never too old to mentor others either. Even if you have to do it a little here and a little there because it's not a major "mentoring season" for you, keep yourself in that giving mode. Receive and give—and receive some more. That's the way it works.

MENTOR PROFILES

As I have said a few times already, I love to be around people who intimidate me to greatness. I love to be around people who are more anointed than I am, someone who knows more Bible than I do, someone who prays more often and more powerfully than I do. What I have learned is that sometimes I need to just go on in, sit down at his or her feet, and let the person talk about *me* later. By nature, I am very bashful (that is, unless the anointing hits me), so it takes me a little while, but after some time, I usually come around to being able to speak up.

You need to be persistent if you want to find mentors who will truly sharpen you. (The Bible says in Proverbs 27:17, "As iron sharpens iron, so a man sharpens the countenance of his friend.") It can be a challenge to find the right kind of person.

You may need to go to considerable trouble to make contact with a potential mentor, but keep asking for an appointment until you get one. Don't let geographical distance become a barrier; get in your car or grab a bus ticket or an airplane ticket, and go wher-

> TAKE STOCK OF WHATEVER YOU NEED TO LEARN ABOUT, AND THEN FIND A WAY TO GET AROUND PEOPLE WHO CAN TEACH YOU.

ever you need to go. If you can hook up with someone who is a good match for you and who can guide you into your destiny, then it's worth any amount of trouble and expense to make it happen. Let me add a word of advice: Always call and make an appointment. Never show up unannounced. No one likes those kinds of surprises.

Take stock of whatever you need to learn about, and then find a way to get around people who can teach you. Be around the people who are already living your dreams. If you have a dream to reach your city for God, figure out who is doing that already in their own city, and get into their orbit. If you have a passion for children's ministry, go someplace famous for children's ministry, and learn all you can. Find people's Web sites; get ahold of their phone numbers; use e-mail. If you're trying to connect with someone who has a big church or a big ministry, find out the name of the administrative assistant, and call often until you can get through to the person you want. The idea is to go and hook yourself up with people who are doing what you want to do and who are doing it with excellence. Study their methods. Ask them questions.

Paul said, "Pattern yourselves after me [follow my example], as I imitate and follow Christ (the Messiah)" (1 Cor. 11:1, AMP). You have to have somebody to follow. If you look and pursue long enough, you will succeed. You may feel like Elijah did when he thought he was the only one on the face of the earth who had not bowed his knee to Baal (1 Kings 19). But God is saying to you just as He said to Elijah, "Get up and go. I have seven thousand who have not bowed their knee to Baal. You're not the only one." You really have to get up and go in order to meet up with your mentors.

DISCERNING AND CONNECTING

Finding mentors is a matter of discernment. For that matter, so is deciding who can and should become your mentee. Both parties often need to seek each other out. It has to be a mutual decision; both mentor and mentee need to agree that this particular mentoring relationship is a good idea. It takes a lot of seeking, and it takes discernment too.

How do you go about discerning such a thing? First, you have to pray and ask God to connect you with the right person or people. Divine appointments will occur. When you meet the right person, you will feel a connection in the spirit, a "knowing." It will be a sense of satisfaction, a tug, or a "click" (that's Bishop T. D. Jakes's term for it).

There will always be people you can hang out with, but they are not going to be your mentors, and you will not be their mentee. With a mentoring relationship, there has to be a connection, or else it won't work. You will be hooked up. You will be headed in the same direction, aiming for the same place. You will be able to tell that you have similar destinies. The other person will have a faith like yours. The other person's anointing will be comparable to the one you have (or want to have). As I have said already, the relationship will have elements of parenting in it. You will recognize a "family resemblance" in your spiritual mentor, and your mentor will recognize it too. He or she will be able to "mother" or "father" you more easily because of that similarity.

I can hear your questions about this: Where do you look for people? What if you can't actually find somebody? How can you figure out if you can "click" if you can't find somebody in the first place? One thing I can say is that the people you hear about the most may not be the right ones. You will find that the majority of leaders in the church are not geared toward mentoring. But that doesn't mean that you will search in vain. The mentors are out there. Ask the Lord to guide you, and ask Him to open your eyes. Be specific. "Seek, and ye *shall* find" (Matt. 7:7, KJV).

Don't rule out the possibility that you may end up with several mentors all at one time. At the least, you may have a series of mentors as you progress through the seasons of your life. You are not necessarily looking for only one individual who will become a lifelong guru-type person to guide you from now on.

To repeat my line about dead people—you may decide that your best mentor is someone who is literally dead! It's not unusual to derive a great deal of mentoring from the writings or recordings of people who are long gone. In a similar way, you may decide to consider someone who has a public ministry and can be your "mentor from afar." Who doesn't know of people like this? That well-known person will not consider you a mentee, but a form of mentoring can take place anyway.

As you search, take a good look at the *fruit* of a person's life. Is it sweet, or is it bitter? Giftedness is important, and status can be important, but they do not supersede the importance of character and the fruit of the Spirit (love, joy, peace, patience, and so on). Take a long look at the person's character traits. How does he or she act when the pressure is on? What kinds of things does this person talk about in casual conversation? Does this person cultivate friendships and healthy relationships with other people, or is he or she isolated and perhaps out of touch with real-life issues? Look at your potential mentor's actions and behavior, and pay attention to the people who surround him or her.

> ONE WARNING: DO *NOT* HOOK UP WITH INDEPENDENT SELF-PROCLAIMED "MENTORS" WHO WANT A FOLLOWING.

Whether you're considering people who might be able to mentor you, or whether you are deciding about mentoring others, take my advice, and don't move too fast. You might make the same mistake Paul and Barnabas evidently made when they included John Mark in their mission trip. (See Acts 15.) John Mark had been a mentee of one or both of these men. So far, so good. Then they decided to take him along on the trip, and there was something about that trip that he couldn't handle, because he deserted them partway through. It became not only an issue of desertion and having less manpower for that particular trip; it also became a relationship issue between Paul and Barnabas. Barnabas always wanted to think the best of everyone. A lot of us are like that. But Paul was pretty blunt. Paul looked at the fruit of John Mark's life, and he just didn't want to risk another trip with him. He didn't think he could trust him to continue being supportive, and we can assume that he didn't want to put John Mark into any kind of a teaching or mentoring position himself if he hadn't reached the right level of maturity yet. Barnabas disagreed with Paul, and they had a split in their own relationship for a while. Whatever was the truth about the fruit of John Mark's character, that relationship split was a bitter pill to swallow. At least for a period of time, the fruit coming from John Mark's life was not good. You can tell a lot about a person by paying attention to the fruit of his or her life. Jesus said:

> You will know them by their fruits. Do men gather grapes from thornbushes or figs from thistles? Even so, every good tree bears good fruit, but a bad tree bears bad fruit. A good tree cannot bear bad fruit, nor can a bad tree bear good fruit. Every tree that does not bear good fruit is cut down and thrown into the fire. Therefore by their fruits you will know them.
> —Matthew 7:16–20

What I'm saying is when you're looking for a mentor, take a careful look at the fruit of this person's life. Is it good fruit or bad fruit (or hard-to-tell fruit)? Is this the same fruit that you want in your life? Does this person put others under uncomfortable pressure? Do you feel built up and encouraged when you are around this person, or do you feel uncertain and inferior? Look for telltale warning signs, but also look for encouraging signs. Don't be too cynical and suspicious, even as you also avoid being too naïve and idealistic.

One warning: do *not* hook up with independent self-proclaimed "mentors" who want a following. (This can be especially true of prophetic mentoring.) Is your potential mentor under authority in a house of God? You will reflect whatever is being released into you. You don't want to be reflecting something that comes from the enemy's camp. As Mike Murdock says, "Satan's favorite entry point into your life is always through someone close to you."[1] Don't let that someone be your mentor.

Again and again, ask God to guide you. He will answer your prayers. He knows every hair on your head, and He wants to make it possible for you to grow and thrive. He loves to connect people so that the body of believers can be healthy and strong.

What If It Doesn't Work?

Mentoring is a little bit like investment; there's a risk involved. Instead of money, you're investing yourself in someone else, or you are allowing someone else to invest in you. Sometimes, in spite of your best efforts to make a good investment, it doesn't work out. Has this happened to you? How can you work out this kind of a situation?

Let's say you have established a mentoring relationship with someone. You mentor this person. You talk with and share your life for a while. You realize once it is too late that you don't have a mentee; you have a "parasite" on your hands. This is a very uncomfortable situation. The person demands too much of your time and expects results that are too quick. He or she is taking this persistence thing to an extreme. You're feeling besieged and trapped. Here's some strongly worded advice from Rick Renner:

> Each time you open the door to those treasures and begin to share them with someone else, you need to remember that you're sharing your *pearls* with that person. The counsel and advice you're giving may be free to him, but it has cost you everything! So if what you are sharing isn't appreciated, *stop giving that person your pearls!*...Jesus uses the example of "swine" or "pigs" to describe this category of people who couldn't care less about what you are trying to tell them. The word "swine" is from the Greek word *choipos*, and it can be translated as *pig, sow, swine,* or *hog*....For Jesus to refer to people as swine was a very powerful and graphic depiction! Pigs are consumers....Driven to have their need for food met, pigs never stop to say thank you to the person who brought it to them....This is exactly like people who don't appreciate the holy things that are freely given to them from the depths of another person's life. It's sad to say, but many believers live and act just like pigs because they are careless, mindless consumers of other people's time and energy.[2]

That's what can happen sometimes. Mercifully, it doesn't happen all the time. But you need to know that it's OK to pull out of a mentoring relationship if you can't work through the problems in it. Some people are just freeloaders, and you don't want to be saddled with them. They want you to carry them all the time. They don't understand that we are each supposed to stand on our own two feet in the kingdom of God. "For each one shall bear his own load" (Gal. 6:5). It can be difficult to say no to such people. Often you feel sorry for them, and you truly would like to help them out. Sometimes you've already committed so much time and effort to them that your own sense of responsibility makes you want to carry through the thing you've begun.

Some of these people are dead in a way that I *can't* work with. When I said I like to work with dead people, what I meant was people who are dead to their own flesh and free to become all that God wants them to become. But there's another kind of dead—dead in heart. These people can't be nurtured. It doesn't matter how wonderful you are or how much you prod them. They're dead to your efforts. They can't really respond. They're satisfied with what they have already. They think that growing in Christ looks like a lot of hard work, and they'd like you to do it for them.

Now Jesus has some peculiar sheep, and you might even be one of them. That's not what I'm talking about here. *Peculiar* doesn't have to mean "bad." Mentoring might work out fine with someone who is a little unusual, even with a sheep who has gone astray in some ways. Take my advice as your mentor for this moment (while you're reading my book)—risk the investment. Invest yourself in others, and make as good an investment as you can. Use your own common sense, and trust God for the details.

GO FOR THE FRUIT THAT LASTS

Your goal is good fruit. You want good fruit to come from your life, and you want to sow and produce good fruit in the lives of others. Mentoring will produce *some* kind of fruit. It might be good, and it might be bad. I don't need to tell you that the world does not need any more *bad* fruit. So keep your eye on the fruit. Make sure it's good.

If you have found someone to mentor you, ask God to bless the fruit of your relationship. Do not be like the parasite mentee who was described above. Don't be too passive or take your mentor for granted. But don't pester him or her mercilessly either. Do not expect your mentor to do the hard work of making you grow. That's your job. Make your spirit receptive, like a fertile field. Feed and water what gets planted there. Don't forget to share some of the new fruit with your mentor as well as with others.

> GOD VERY MUCH WANTS US TO BE RIGHTLY RELATED TO EACH OTHER SO THAT HIS BODY CAN FUNCTION AT ITS BEST.

If you become a mentor, make careful decisions about whom you will take care of in a mentoring relationship. Throughout, keep your eye on the fruit. Is this relationship going somewhere? Are problems getting ironed out well? Are you communicating well? Can you tell if your mentee is learning from you? Can you honestly say that you love your mentee with the love of Jesus?

You are sowing into the life of this person. You are reproducing the fruit that exists in your own life. If you sow good seed and you sow it well, in good soil, the harvest will be plentiful. You have a job before you. You may not see instant results, so be patient, just as the farmer is patient over the field he has planted (James 5:7).

The seed you sow, like farmer's seed, must be buried before it can grow up into fruitfulness. But you can rest easy about the outcome if you sow generously and well. Let the words of Jesus encourage you:

> Unless I die I will be alone—a single seed. But my death will produce many new wheat kernels—a plentiful harvest of new lives.
>
> —John 12:24, TLB

> For the man who uses well what he is given shall be given more.
>
> —Matthew 25:29, TLB

> Your care for others is the measure of your greatness.
>
> —Luke 9:48, TLB

Those words are true if the mentoring relationship is a healthy one. If, however, you decide that it is not going well, and you decide that you need to cut back on your commitment or even terminate the relationship, ask the Holy Spirit to help you figure out what to do. He is your Counselor, and He will advise you. Jesus, the Great Shepherd of the sheep, cares about every individual in His flock. He very much wants us to be rightly related to each other so that His body can function at its best. As Rod Parsley says, "Although you are complete in Christ, you must be joined to the Body of Christ to be functionally complete and to accomplish His will."[3] The key is to be *rightly* joined. Here's how the New Living Translation describes this:

> He makes the whole body fit together perfectly. As each part does its own special work, it helps the other parts grow, so that the whole body is healthy and growing and full of love.
>
> —Ephesians 4:16, NLT

To be rightly joined as parts of the body of Christ, should your relationship be a mentoring relationship—or not? In your own body, your eyebrows can't usually "mentor" your earlobes.

In 1 Kings, we read a statement that King David made to his son Solomon. He said, "I am going where every man on earth must some day go. I'm counting on you to be a strong and worthy successor" (1 Kings 2:2, TLB). To you who are reading this book, I'm saying that I'm counting on you to be a strong and worthy successor—not just to your mentors, but also to the Father, who has entrusted you with gifts. It goes back to the story of the good stewards. (See Matthew 25.) They were given gifts: five talents, two talents, and one talent. Like the good stewards, who were good investors and wise risk takers, we too need to be good stewards of what God has given us.

I have said that I love to be around people who intimidate me to greatness. I didn't say I love to be around people who intimidate me. I love to be around people who spur me on to great things. I love to be around a Marilyn Hickey, who intimidates me to memorize the Word. I love to sit at the feet of a great preacher whose words blow my socks off. I love to be around people who have such great faith that they encourage me to have more faith. You are the same way, I hope.

Get around some great saints of God and gather others around yourself. It's never too late. You were made to mentor.

> Two are better than one, because they have a good [more satisfying] reward for their labor; for if they fall, the one will lift up his fellow. But woe to him who is alone when he falls and has not another to lift him up! Again, if two lie down together, then they have warmth; but how can one be warm alone? And though a man might prevail against him who is alone, two will withstand him. A threefold cord is not quickly broken.
>
> —Ecclesiastes 4:9–12, AMP

CHAPTER 9

THE GUMPTION TO GO!

G UMPTION IS A very interesting word. It could be used to describe someone who has "guts" or nerve or courage. It makes me think of the saying, "Faith is courage that has said its prayers." If you don't miss your moment and you walk on in faith to meet it, you have the "gumption to go."

Someone who did not miss her moment and who had some gumption too was the incomparable Rosa Parks. She was the African American civil rights activist whom the U.S. Congress later called the "mother of the modern-day civil rights movement." On December 1, 1955, Parks refused to obey bus driver James Blake's order that she give up her seat to make room for a white passenger. This action of civil disobedience started the Montgomery bus boycott, which became one of the largest movements against racial segregation. Rosa has a lasting worldwide legacy. She never gave up. She definitely had some gumption about her.

Someone else comes to mind: Albert Einstein. When he was young, Albert's speech was severely delayed. He did not begin to talk until he was three. In addition, he suffered from dyslexia. After he moved to a different type of school, his academic performance improved dramatically, and before too long he was going so fast and excelling so much that his teachers could not keep up with him. As you know, Albert Einstein grew up to become one of the greatest physicists and scientists of the twentieth century. That takes a lot of gumption. In fact, *TIME* magazine named him the most important person in the twentieth century.

Then there's Abraham Lincoln, who was a true "gumptor." You've probably seen this discouraging list of his early "accomplishments":

- In 1831, he lost his job.
- In 1832, he was defeated in a run for the Illinois state legislature.
- In 1833, he failed in business.
- In 1835, his sweetheart died.
- In 1836, he had a nervous breakdown.
- In 1843, he was defeated for nomination for the U.S. Congress.
- In 1846, he was finally elected to Congress.
- In 1848, he lost renomination.
- In 1849, he was rejected for a land officer position.
- In 1855, he was defeated in a run for the U.S. Senate.
- In 1856, he was defeated in a run for nomination for U.S. vice president.
- In 1859, he was defeated again in a run for the U.S. Senate.
- In 1860, he was elected U.S. president.[1]

Now, ladies and gentlemen, this was a man who most definitely did not quit until his *moment* finally came! You talk about some *gumption*. He had it.

Peter was also a "gumptor." Peter had a very interesting life after he met Jesus. Whether it was walking on water (Matt. 14), going up the mountain to see Jesus transfigured (Matt. 17; Mark 9; Luke 9), or tangling with the crowd in the Garden of Gethsemane (Matt. 26; Mark 14; Luke 22; John 18), Peter was 100 percent involved. He didn't always do the right thing. He was impulsive by nature, and that got him into trouble more than once. (I'm thinking of Matthew 26:34: "Before the rooster crows, you will deny Me three times.") But he always rallied. He always came around. Jesus even made sure that he was restored after he had denied Him, allowing Peter to be one of the first people to see the empty tomb and, in the most touching moment of them all, talking with him one-on-one on the beach and telling him, "Feed My lambs.... Tend My sheep.... Feed My sheep" (John 21:15–17).

> TO MAKE YOUR MOMENT COUNT, YOU NEED TO BE LIKE PETER; YOU NEED TO MAKE SURE THAT YOU HAVE THE "GO YE."

You could say that Peter's life consisted of an amazing series of God moments. And because so many of them are described in the Bible, we can see how he responded to them. We know about the ones he missed as well as the ones he didn't. Peter's life as a disciple and a follower of Jesus pulls open the curtains to reveal something very special—the incredible way the Lord Himself makes every effort to help Peter—and us—connect with Him.

After Jesus's resurrection, Peter followed the Holy Spirit, and he had many more adventures. He had gotten a lot better at listening to the Spirit instead of forging ahead under his own steam. Even so, more than once he might have missed his moment to act if the Lord

Himself hadn't sent help. For instance, remember what happened when he was locked up in prison?

> Peter was therefore kept in prison, but constant prayer was offered to God for him by the church. And when Herod was about to bring him out, that night Peter was sleeping, bound with two chains between two soldiers; and the guards before the door were keeping the prison. Now behold, an angel of the Lord stood by him, and a light shone in the prison; and he struck Peter on the side and raised him up, saying, "Arise quickly!" And his chains fell off his hands. Then the angel said to him, "Gird yourself and tie on your sandals"; and so he did. And he said to him, "Put on your garment and follow me." So he went out and followed him, and did not know that what was done by the angel was real, but thought he was seeing a vision. When they were past the first and the second guard posts, they came to the iron gate that leads to the city, which opened to them of its own accord; and they went out and went down one street, and immediately the angel departed from him.
>
> —Acts 12:5–10

That was quite a God moment, and Peter did not miss it. (Neither would I if an angel struck me on my side and ordered me to my feet!) God made sure of it. Because of God's power, Peter had the gumption to go and do something that otherwise would have been very foolish to try, not to mention impossible to achieve. Nobody just gets up and walks out of prison scot-free like that. With God's angel leading him, Peter did.

That is encouraging to me personally. Even strong and forceful Peter might have missed that moment of escape and deliverance if he had been left to his own devices. There really was precious little he could have done in his own strength to get out of that situation. You see, along with an angelic encounter, God sent Peter the courage and obedience and faith and just plain *gumption* that would be required to follow through. Another way to look at it is to say that God most definitely gave Peter what I call the "go ye" that he needed.

(Notice, however, that in the midst of all the supernatural shakings and quakings, Peter had to bend over and put on his own sandals and pull his clothes on by himself. He had to move on his own. The angel didn't clothe him supernaturally and transport him out of the dungeon in a fiery chariot.)

Although he thought it was a dream at first, Peter walked out of there on his own two feet. He didn't worry about the next locked door ahead. He didn't spend any time looking over his shoulder for the guards' pursuit. He just proceeded out with the angel in the lead. And when the angel disappeared, he carried on alone, walking to his friends' house without an escort. Don't you think Peter had to have some extra gumption in order to get up and go like that? That's what this chapter is about—getting the strength from God that follows a call from Him.

When a moment of God's call comes to you, you may or may not be in some kind of a prison. It may happen to you when you're running a load of clothes in the wash or driving down the street in your car. I don't think you will have very much trouble recognizing God's touch if you have gotten very far in your life and if you have gotten this far in this book. In other words, you probably will not miss your moment.

However, to make your moment count, you need to be like Peter; you need to make sure that you have the "go ye." You need to make sure you have not only your marching orders and a sense of anointing, but also the courage to go forth and do whatever God has called you to do. To make sure your God moment doesn't just blow away in the wind and land somewhere else, you need to exercise the right combination of obedience and anointing. You need to get up on your own two feet and put on your shoes (of faith), and then you need to follow the leading of the Holy Spirit as obediently as you possibly can, asking for more of God's help every step of the way. As you do so, amazing things will start to happen. The purposes of God will start to be realized in and through your life.

Gumptionless

The children of Israel provide us with a negative example of what I'm talking about. They lacked the gumption to go. From early on, they grumbled and complained. They compared their life as nomads to their more "secure" life as slaves in Egypt. They got tired of manna. They let those giants in the land deter them.

In spite of all the evidence of God's supernatural intervention on their behalf, they refused to follow Him wholeheartedly. As a result, they had to wander for forty long years in the desert. God kept them alive (well, most of them) and their sandals didn't wear out. But a whole generation missed its moment of victorious liberation and unmitigated blessing. They missed it because they didn't have the gumption to go.

Have I Missed My Moment?

Do you sometimes wonder if you have missed your moment as the Israelites did? Do you wonder if you missed a "big one"? What if you have married the wrong person? What if you have given away everything you own and moved to another city and started a ministry, and now you're in a lot of trouble?

What I'm trying to say in this final chapter is that God will give you the grace you need in whatever form you need it in. He will keep you from missing your moment if at all possible, and He will give you the strength you need to follow through. He will give you a second (or third or fourth) chance if necessary. He will help you. He loves you. You are His child.

So back to your question. If you think you have missed a "big one," or even a small one, go back to what you think made you miss it. What made you get off track? What made you respond the way you did? You will not be able to revise your whole history, but you can learn something from your mistakes, and you won't have to repeat your history. Very often, God will show you how He intends to use you right where you have ended up. You think you married the wrong person? Don't just get a divorce. Wait and pray. This difficult marriage may become your greatest moment yet. You need to hear from God. Let your desperation drive you to Him. Go back to whatever made you miss your moment.

Remember, you do have an adversary, and he does prowl around looking for someone to devour (1 Pet. 5:8). You may have listened to him instead of to God. The devil is *not* your friend. With all his stony heart, he wants you to fail. He wants you to miss your moment—or to think you have missed it. He wants to interfere with God's plans and destiny for your life. He has a whole arsenal of tricks. (And he's not very original, just malicious. So it's easy to identify those tricks.) Some common ways the devil will try to trip you up include discouragement, regrets, disobedience, sin, faith problems, and weakness. We'll talk about each of those in this chapter.

Don't Let Discouragement Make You Miss Your Moment

You have to stand strong against the devil. You have to come against every device and every plan of the enemy that would try to take you away from what God has said. You have to understand your authority in Christ and use it.

I love Barney in *The Andy Griffith Show*. I love to watch the reruns. Have you ever seen that episode where a big ol' guy comes up against little, puny Barney. Barney is looking up at him with his owly eyes. Then he stands up as straight as he can, and he says, "Let me tell you something. You are a lot bigger than I am. But one thing you've got to remember is what this badge right here represents."

> THE ONLY WAY I KNOW HOW TO DEFEAT THE DEVIL'S DISCOURAGEMENT AND FEAR IS TO SPEAK OUT THE OPPOSITE.

Barney had the authority. He was the sheriff's deputy. He went on to say, "This badge represents this county. It represents the people of this county. It represents the state of North Carolina. So if you come against me, you're coming against the whole state of North Carolina!"

When the devil comes against you, you are not by yourself!

Well, you say, "Judy, how about you? Don't you get discouraged sometimes? Do you *always* feel this boldness coming on you?" You know, there are times when I walk out on stage and I don't feel the boldness at all. But I have to believe that God is going to be there with me. I have to believe that He is with me. He'll never leave me and never forsake me.

Sometimes I just start off, "Oh, Jesus. Oh, God." Especially when I go into a church. I've become kind of a professional feeler when it comes to feeling out the atmosphere in a place. I can walk through a front door and start praying in tongues immediately: "Oh, Jesus! Help me today, Lord. Whew! It's going to be me and You today, Lord." There are other places where I walk in and think, "I'm going to have to catch up, because these people are way ahead of me, and I've got to run as fast as I can to catch up with them." But either way, the boldness, the power, and the authority of God will rise up inside me. I'll begin to preach and proclaim Him. And the glory of God comes. The anointing comes and saturates me. The boldness and the authority and the power and the anointing of God connect together, and I come out of myself. I feel like I come right out of my feet of clay sometimes, and God shows up.

My part is to put my shoulders back and straighten my back and lift my head up as high as my faith. I have to know whom I represent. I don't walk onto that stage *acting* like I have it together. I walk out there because when I do, He will bring it together. I have prepared and fasted and prayed, and now it's time. I'm ready. Not by my might. Not by my power, but by His Spirit. I depend on the Lord because I'm doing what He told me to do.

The only way I know how to defeat the devil's discouragement and fear is to speak out the opposite. I stand up in the authority of God Himself and make pronouncements of truth. "Thou shalt also decree a thing, and it shall be established unto thee: and the light shall shine upon thy ways" (Job 22:28, KJV). When a king decrees a thing, it shall be *established* because of his authority. Nothing can stop it. Nothing can hinder it. Nothing can deter it or delete it. It's really true that the power of life and death is in your mouth. You are backed up by all the authority in heaven, which is a lot bigger than the state of North Carolina.

APPLE OF HIS EYE

You know how it is when you get some grit in your eye? Your eye waters and stings, and that little speck irritates you until you stop everything and get it out. It's the same way for God. *You* are the "apple of his eye" (Deut. 32:10; Zech. 2:8). The devil may kick up some dust, but when God detects the first hint of injury, He rises up to defend you. On your right side is the Father. On the left side is Jesus, your elder brother. In front of you is the Holy Spirit. And around you are the angels that surround you day and night. You are not by yourself. The devil wants you to think that you are by yourself. He wants to make you discouraged, fatigued, and confused. But you are not alone, not by any means.

The Holy Spirit will rise up in you and you will be bold to sing or preach or testify. You'll get bold to write a letter or write a book. You'll get bold enough to see the thing through. Every mountain shall be made low and every valley shall be filled in. Every crooked path shall be made straight, because you're walking in authority.

You have to expect opposition to your mission. I have said this many times, and I will keep saying it. Whenever you step out and begin to walk in obedience to God, there is going to be some kind of opposition from the devil. Jesus faced it, and so will you. You won't necessarily be led out into the wilderness as He was (Matt. 4:1; Mark 1:12; Luke 4:1), because the devil attacks people in many ways. Today, it may be a fearsome medical diagnosis. Tomorrow it may be the loss of employment. Next year, it may be trouble with one of your kids. Sometimes it's just sort of generalized anxieties, sleeplessness, stress, or overall discouragement.

Whatever you do, learn to recognize discouragement as the opposite of God. Will God ever discourage you? Absolutely not. Even when things are tough all around, He *encourages* you, which means He puts *heart* into you. If something is sapping your "gumption to go," you can assume that the devil is messing around with you.

The goal isn't to escape all the opposition. No, the trials and tribulations and wilderness times are part of what we signed up for. They are inevitable. God will allow as many of them as you can handle, and part of the reason is so that you will learn to rely on Him alone, not on your own strength.

The goal is to prevail. You can't become a victor if you don't have something to become victorious over. Adversities are part of the deal. Expect them. Accept them. Keep looking to Jesus for all the strength and encouragement you need.

EXPECT ADVERSITY

Remember how it was with Mary, the mother of Jesus? She was not very old in years when the angel came to tell her that she was going to get pregnant with the Son of God. That announcement did not land her on the front cover of *TIME* magazine. Instead, it branded her as an immoral woman. She never asked for so much trouble. But when her moment came, she did not miss it, and she carried through with all the gumption God gave her, bravely carrying her baby to term, traveling on a donkey at the end of her pregnancy because of the census, giving birth in a barn, and before the baby Jesus was very old, running to another country with Joseph to protect Him from Herod. This whole thing was not easy in the least. It was not glamorous, no matter how many pretty Christmas cards you have seen with her picture on them.

It kept going like that for the rest of her life. She lost Jesus once when He was twelve years old, and then apparently she lost Joseph to death, and she became a widow. She finished raising her Son alone, and about the time He became well established in His father's carpentry business, He took off as an itinerant rabbi. She and the rest of the family weren't always sure that what He was doing was the right thing (Matt. 12:46–47; Mark 3:31–33; Luke 8:19–20). Eventually, she had to watch the most agonizing thing any mother can watch—the execution of her firstborn Son, with all of the blood and suffering that it entailed. She did not run away from it. She did not collapse. She was still there in the Upper Room (Acts 1:14).

> DISCOURAGEMENT AND REGRETS ARE CLOSE COUSINS. IF YOU GET TOO INVOLVED WITH EITHER ONE OF THEM, YOU CAN EASILY MISS A MOVE OF GOD.

Through all of that, as far as we know, Mary's God moments were few and far between. She had to have the wherewithal to go forward on the strength of what the Father had spoken to her in her infrequent encounters with Him. Through His prophet Simeon, He said, "Yes, a sword will pierce through your own soul also" (Luke 2:35), and she accepted it as truth. She didn't grumble and moan. She didn't compare herself with her sister, who I'm sure had a much more normal life than she did. She didn't let the changing circumstances and the raw emotions throw her off track. She had said yes back when the angel visited the first time, and she meant it. God gave her the grace, and she used it. Mary had the divine "go-ye gumption" that comes with a call from God, and she trusted in Him every step of the way.

Remember how it was with Paul too. For all the years of his life as a Christian, Paul was continually suffering from something. He had multiple dangers from traveling. He was often nearly overcome by fatigue, hunger, or plain old discouragement: "We were so utterly and unbearably weighed down and crushed that we despaired even of life [itself]" (2 Cor. 1:8, AMP).

But like Mary, Paul accepted all the trials and adversities as part of the package, and he learned to rejoice in them. We're supposed to learn the same thing so that at the end of our lives, we can say with Paul, "I have fought the good fight, I have finished the race, I have kept the faith" (2 Tim. 4:7).

Remember—the same power that raised Christ Jesus from the dead is in you! The same power that got Him up from the grave is going to get you up and give you the gumption to go and do the thing He is calling you to do.

DON'T LET REGRETS MAKE YOU MISS YOUR MOMENT

Discouragement and regrets are close cousins. If you get too involved with either one of them, you can easily miss a move of God. With regrets, you can get stuck in backward thinking. You can stall out in all of the "what ifs" or the "if onlys": "What if I had accepted the first job that I was offered?" "If only I had decided to get some education first." "What if I hadn't gotten pregnant?" "If only I had any idea how to raise a child." "What if I have ruined my chances for the future?" "If only I had listened to my mother."

What's the point of doing that? We all slip into regrets from time to time, but when you stop and think about it, what do they accomplish? I don't think they even help us learn how to do it better the next time. Regrets are dead ends on the road of life.

Does the Bible talk about regrets? You bet it does. Listen to Paul:

> I don't mean to say I am perfect. I haven't learned all I should even yet, but I keep working toward that day when I will finally be all that Christ saved me for and wants me to be.
>
> No, dear brothers, I am still not all I should be, but I am bringing all my energies to bear on this one thing: Forgetting the past and looking forward to what lies ahead, I strain to reach the end of the race and receive the prize for which God is calling us up to heaven because of what Christ Jesus did for us.
>
> —Philippians 3:12–14, TLB

Paul, of all people, could have been overwhelmed with regrets. Before meeting Jesus on the road to Damascus, when he was still called Saul, he had spent all his energy persecuting Christians to the death:

> Saul shamefully treated and laid waste the church continuously [with cruelty and violence]; and entering house after house, he dragged out men and women and committed them to prison.
>
> —Acts 8:3, AMP

He even stood by approvingly when Stephen was being stoned to death (Acts 7:58). Nothing he could do now would bring people's loved ones back. They were dead. Regrets could have swamped him. And yet he says he's now pouring all his energy into one thing: "forgetting the past and looking forward to what lies ahead." In other words, he decided to dispense with regrets.

You can apply that same wisdom to your own regrets. You may not have dragged men and women out of their homes, but (unless you are currently very young) you have most likely done quite a few things you regret doing. When you see some of the repercussions of your bad decisions, you shrink inside. Something about it puts everything on "pause." You stop moving. You can't move forward as long as you're looking over your shoulder.

What's behind you? You can forget about it. It's in the past, and you can't change it now. You can put all those things into God's hands and ask Him to restore to you whatever the devil has stolen. Don't get stalled in regrets. You can forget about your failed marriage, your financial mistakes, your parenting errors, the problems you have caused with your health or weight. You can start fresh. You can declare, "Today I will declare the end from the

> YOUR ABILITY TO OBEY IS PART OF GOD'S GRACE TOWARD YOU.

beginning, as I forget yesterday and move into my future. I will not allow the distraction of looking at the past cause me to miss enjoying the adventure of *now*!"[2]

If Paul could put all his energy into forgetting his raging, murder-filled past, surely you will be able to apply yourself to forgetting your sins and faults and mistakes. Don't let your regrets steal your present moment. In particular, don't let them make you miss your present moment with God.

History will repeat itself over and over again, but God has something to say about what you're going to do. Today you have the power to declare the end from the beginning, but you have to put the past behind you. You can't look at what other people have done, said, or accomplished. You have to look at where God is taking *you*. You have to move into the future, which is another way of saying you have to move into your destiny. God is always in the *now*. He is the *I Am*. He is not the "I Was." He is not the God of the dead; He is the God of the living.

Solomon observed:

> What is happening now has happened before, and what will happen in the future has happened before, because God makes the same things happen over and over again.
>
> —Ecclesiastes 3:15, NLT

> The LORD has made everything for his own purposes.
>
> —Proverbs 16:4, NLT

> We can make our own plans, but the LORD gives the right answer.
>
> —Proverbs 16:1, NLT

DON'T LET DISOBEDIENCE AND SIN MAKE YOU MISS YOUR MOMENT

If you obey God from your first realization that He is calling you to do something, your obedience will guarantee that you will have all the resources, confidence, anointing, and authority you need to achieve His will. Even your ability to obey is part of God's grace toward you. Paul said, "If I proclaim the Message, it's not to get something out of it for myself. I'm compelled to do it, and doomed if I don't!" (1 Cor. 9:16, THE MESSAGE). Paul knew that if he did not obey what was compelling him forward, he would not have the ability to do it at all.

Speaking about the Israelites, the psalm writer says:

> [God] led forth his own people like a flock, guiding them safely through the wilderness.... Yet though he did all this for them, they still rebelled against the God above all gods and refused to follow his commands. They turned back from entering the Promised Land and disobeyed as their fathers had. *Like a crooked arrow, they missed the target of God's will.*
> —Psalm 78:52, 56–57, TLB, emphasis added

Paul obeyed, whereas his Israelite ancestors did not. We should take this as a solemn warning. God takes obedience seriously. Moses preached about it to the people of Israel:

> Let no one blithely think..."I shall prosper even though I walk in my own stubborn way!"....
>
> "Why has the Lord done this to his land?" the nations will ask. "Why was he so angry?"
>
> And they will be told, "Because the people of the land broke the contract made with them by Jehovah, the God of their ancestors, when he brought them out of the land of Egypt. For they worshiped other gods, violating his express command. That is why the anger of the Lord was hot against this land, so that all his curses (which are recorded in this book) broke forth upon them. In great anger the Lord rooted them out of their land and threw them away into another land, where they live today!"

> There are secrets the Lord your God has not revealed to us,
> but *these words that he has revealed are for us and our children
> to obey forever.*
> —Deuteronomy 29:19, 24–29, TLB, emphasis added

I'm telling you, you are called. Don't miss your moment to respond to each part of God's call. You need to listen and obey because He has spotlighted you. You don't need further affirmation. You don't need further confirmation. You especially don't need acclamation. You just need to listen and obey and do what God has asked you to do. Yield yourself to the Spirit of God. He is going to reveal Himself. Leave everything else behind; leave it there, and forget about who and what you once were. Focus on Him, and be free in the Spirit. If you obey, God can do great and mighty things with you.

Don't Let Faith Problems Make You Miss Your Moment

God *will* give you a vision and a call if you ask Him to. He will renew His call if He needs to. It's *His*, after all, so He definitely keeps it in mind. Waiting for your vision to be fulfilled takes patience because it may take awhile to flesh out the details. But patience is not the same as indifference. In fact, patience conveys the idea of someone who is tremendously strong and able to withstand all assaults—with faith in the One who is in charge.

Habakkuk prophesied:

> For the vision is yet for an appointed time; but at the end it shall speak, and not lie: though it tarry, wait for it; because it will surely come, it will not tarry. Behold, his soul which is

lifted up is not upright in him: but the just shall live by his
faith.

—Habakkuk 2:3–4, KJV

The Word of God declares that the Lord has dealt each person
a measure of faith. (See Romans 12:3.) There is great faith, strong
faith, weak faith, and being full of faith. You may be one of those
with weak faith, but you do have *some* faith. Put it in the right place.
Put your faith in the Lord.

LET DESPERATION DRIVE YOUR FAITH

Imagine for a moment what it must have been like to be one of the
children of Israel who had just been liberated from Egypt. Most of
them probably didn't know the whole story about Moses and the
burning bush, but they knew they were walking in the midst of one
of God's miracles.

Then they came smack up against the shore of the Red Sea. What
now, Moses? Everybody came to a complete halt. People stopped
milling around. Mothers hushed their babies. They were trapped!
Now they could actually hear the Egyptian chariots galloping in
their direction. They could see the clouds of dust rising in the
distance.

> The children of Israel lifted their eyes, and behold, the Egyp-
> tians marched after them. So they were very afraid, and the
> children of Israel cried out to the LORD. Then they said to
> Moses, "Because there were no graves in Egypt, have you
> taken us away to die in the wilderness? Why have you so dealt
> with us, to bring us up out of Egypt? Is this not the word that
> we told you in Egypt, saying, 'Let us alone that we may serve

the Egyptians?' For it would have been better for us to serve the Egyptians than that we should die in the wilderness."

And Moses said to the people, "Do not be afraid. Stand still, and see the salvation of the Lord, which He will accomplish for you today. For the Egyptians whom you see today, you shall see again no more forever. The Lord will fight for you, and you shall hold your peace."

And the Lord said to Moses, "Why do you cry to Me? Tell the children of Israel to go forward. But lift up your rod, and stretch out your hand over the sea and divide it. And the children of Israel shall go on dry ground through the midst of the sea.

—Exodus 14:10–16

The people had no choice. They were so desperate. Moses was desperate too, of course. All of them *had* to put their faith in the word of the Lord. There was nothing else to put their faith in. And their faith was rewarded. God delivered them once more.

Who were they listening to? Who are you listening to? The voice of faith-killing fear? That's the devil every time. The devil *never* tells the truth, so you might as well turn the tables on him. Just take his lies and contradict them. He says, "You're trapped. Look at the Red Sea in front of you. You're doomed." You say, "God is bigger than any Red Sea. Jesus is the way, the truth, and the life. The truth is He'll show me the way through to life."

By the way, God is bigger than the giants in the land too. You might pull together enough faith to surmount the initial obstacles, only to fall down flat in front of "giants" like loneliness, addictions, or poverty. You should know that if you let them intimidate you, your giants will only grow bigger. They aren't going away unless you drive them out. Keep all of your battle gear on at all times, and don't ever forget your shield of faith.

DON'T LET YOUR WEAKNESSES MAKE YOU MISS YOUR MOMENT

I love the flat-out honesty of the Bible. These are real people who encountered God. Some of them missed their encounters, or they didn't follow through afterward. Some did not miss them. Often, it was the same person who did both—miss and not miss. We're all a lot like that.

We've already talked about Peter, who had a pretty good track record overall, considering the magnitude of the God moments he missed (denying the Lord, for example). Of course, most of us don't recognize a missed moment very clearly, and for us, unlike some of Peter's failures, a "missed moment" is not news of biblical proportions. Often enough, we miss the boat because we're still parking the car. We are fallible and inade-

> THE KIND OF STRENGTH THAT GOD PROVIDES IS FORTITUDE FOR YOUR CHARACTER, FOR YOUR WILL.

quate. We are either late for things or we don't show up at all. Just to keep ourselves ready for God, we need a pep talk in order to get pumped up over and over. We need models to emulate, models like Ezekiel and Isaiah and Jesus.

When God called Ezekiel to become a watchman for Israel, He told him, "Behold, I have made your face strong against their faces, and your forehead strong against their foreheads. Like adamant stone, harder than flint, I have made your forehead; do not be afraid of them" (Ezek. 3:8–9). Before that, Isaiah had proclaimed, "Because the Lord God helps me, I will not be dismayed; therefore, I have set my face like flint to do his will, and I know that I will triumph" (Isa. 50:7, TLB). When Jesus knew He was headed for His last days and a painful death, Luke tells us that "He steadfastly set His face to go to Jerusalem" (Luke 9:51).

All of these men, even Jesus, could have chosen otherwise. They were tired already, even exhausted. They had fought many battles and conquered their enemies repeatedly. They were surrounded with supporters who could have taken care of them. They didn't have to put themselves in harm's way. But they did it anyway, out of obedience. They didn't let fear or energy depletion weaken their resolve. They set their faces like flint and pressed through all the obstacles to the final goal. Even when the forces arrayed against them were daunting, they didn't flinch.

They believed that God was enough for them. They didn't forget what He is like:

> The eternal God is your Refuge,
> And underneath are the everlasting arms.
> He thrusts out your enemies before you;
> It is he who cries, "Destroy them!"
> —Deuteronomy 33:27, TLB

The devil knows our weaknesses. He knows. But the good news about that is that our weaknesses are God's strengths. His strength is made perfect in our weakness (2 Cor. 12:10). Whatever God has called you to do, you must do it, because the call of God is without repentance. (See Romans 11:29.) He has put a call on your life, and He has told you, "Go, and I will go with you. My burden is light.

I will be with you, and when the road gets dark, I won't go away. When trouble begins to rise, and when it seems as if you can't do it, remember that My strength is made perfect in your weakness. It's true; in your own strength, you cannot do it. But when your 'natural' puts on My 'super,' it becomes supernatural. And with Me all things become possible. Yes, you can do all things, because I am He who strengthens you."

ALWAYS AN OPEN DOOR

With God, there will always be an open door. Jesus's friend John had walked through a whole lifetime of open doors when he wrote: "I have set before you an open door, and no one can shut it; for you have a little strength, have kept My word, and have not denied My name" (Rev. 3:8). Paul used the same phrase when he wrote to the Corinthians, "There is a wide-open door for a great work here" (1 Cor. 16:9, NLT).

Along with the open door always comes opposition. The second part of Paul's sentence reads, "…although many oppose me." Very few open doors lead straight to heaven. They lead to victories, but only if you persevere. Your open door may not be the open door you were expecting, but it will be open for you, and you can walk through it, counting on God's strength for every step of the way.

You recognize, I hope, that I'm not talking about military strength or even physical strength here. The kind of strength that God provides is fortitude for your character, for your will. He enables you to "set your face like flint." He enables you to stand strong in the face of opposition. He enables you to persevere, even as Elisha did when he followed the steps of his master, Elijah, so that he could be the one to inherit a double portion of his spirit when he was taken up to heaven. (See 2 Kings 2.) That is a pretty good example of somebody not missing his moment.

Later in his life as a prophet, Elisha had to stand by while somebody else almost missed his healing moment because of a character weakness—pride. Do you remember Naaman? He was a military commander for the king of Aram, so he had no shortage of physical strength. However, he did have leprosy, and through a little Israelite slave girl, he heard that Elisha the prophet might be able to heal him. So far, so good. He went to visit Elisha:

> So Naaman went with his horses and chariots and waited at the door of Elisha's house. But Elisha sent a messenger out to him with this message: "Go and wash yourself seven times in the Jordan River. Then your skin will be restored, and you will be healed of your leprosy."
>
> But Naaman became angry and stalked away. "I thought he would certainly come out to meet me!" he said. "I expected him to wave his hand over the leprosy and call on the name of the Lord his God and heal me! Aren't the rivers of Damascus, the Abana and the Pharpar, better than any of the rivers of Israel? Why shouldn't I wash in them and be healed?" So Naaman turned and went away in a rage.
>
> —2 Kings 5:9–12, NLT

Oops! Looks like Naaman missed it! But wait, there's more:

> But his officers tried to reason with him and said, "Sir, if the prophet had told you to do something very difficult, wouldn't you have done it? So you should certainly obey him when he says simply, 'Go and wash and be cured!'" So Naaman went down to the Jordan River and dipped himself seven times, as the man of God had instructed him. And his

skin became as healthy as the skin of a young child's, and he was healed!

Then Naaman and his entire party went back to find the man of God. They stood before him, and Naaman said, "Now I know that there is no God in all the world except in Israel.
—2 Kings 5:13–15, NLT

That was a close call for Naaman. Aren't you glad that God speaks through other people sometimes to make you get back on track? Aren't you glad that you serve a God who is interested in you, who has chosen you, who considers you His special project? Yes, we are weak and fallible. But God takes the initiative with us, time and time again, to make sure we don't miss out. It's for His own glory, you know.

Paul wrote:

For [simply] consider your own call, brethren; not many [of you were considered to be] wise according to human estimates and standards, not many influential and powerful, not many of high and noble birth.

[No] for God selected (deliberately chose) what in the world is foolish to put the wise to shame, and what the world calls weak to put the strong to shame.

And God also selected (deliberately chose) what in the world is lowborn and insignificant and branded and treated with contempt, even the things that are nothing, that He might depose and bring to nothing the things that are, so that no mortal man should [have pretense for glorying and] boast in the presence of God.
—1 Corinthians 1:26–29, AMP

Aren't you glad He "deliberately chose" you? Your significance comes from that choice, which has already been made on your behalf and which does not depend on your qualifications.

I've nearly missed my moment more than once out of complete exhaustion. I have become so overwhelmed that I could not lift a finger. Sometimes I have felt like old Elijah after he prevailed over the prophets of Baal and then ran for his life from Jezebel, only to end up feeling like he was the only prophet on the face of the earth who had remained faithful to God (1 Kings 19). Except at that moment, he wasn't exhibiting much faith. He could have missed his next moment, and I would have understood, because I have been there. I haven't ever called down fire from heaven, but I have been there. I have been so spent that I had nothing left to spend. I have felt as if I have been doing my work and everybody else's too. I have tried to come up with a helpful word from my Bible, only to be able to think of nothing except, "There is no peace...for the wicked" (Isa. 57:21).

> GOD HIMSELF DOES NOT WANT YOU TO MISS YOUR MOMENT. HE WILL DIRECT YOUR FEET ONTO THE RIGHT PATHS. KEEP LOOKING TO HIM

But you know what? God loves us even when we're acting like peevish kids. He has helped me. He told Elijah to get up and go. He has told me the same thing, "Get up!" *Then* and only then, after getting up, has His empowerment started to flow. We can't meet God's moments in our own strength anyway. They require too much of us. We need His Spirit every minute of every day and every minute of every night.

What can you do if you have capitulated to your weakness? You can lay your life back down at His feet. You can decree life back into your dreams. You can get wisdom, whether it's through revelation, mentoring, or lessons learned from your own mistakes.

What moments have you *not* missed? Get around people who can help you hear God. Get back up and get going. God can redeem everything. You may not have missed your moment after all.

God will never, ever leave you an orphan. He says, "I will not leave you orphans; I will come to you" (John 14:18). He will complete what He has begun in your life. With your whole heart, you can believe what the Bible says:

> Looking away [from all that will distract] to Jesus, Who is the Leader and the Source of our faith [giving the first incentive for our belief] and is also its Finisher [bringing it to maturity and perfection].
>
> —Hebrews 12:2, AMP

LET'S NOT MISS OUR MOMENT!

I may be weak and imperfect. I may have to learn everything the hard way. I may not sing like CeCe. (Brother, I wish I could!) I may not be able to expound the truth the way Joseph Garlington can, taking one word and preaching a whole sermon about it. I may not be able to do all the things that other people can do.

But I can be the best Judy Jacobs Tuttle that God has put on this earth. I can be faithful to what He has called and anointed me to be. I can be faithful in being the wife and mother He's called me to be. I can be faithful in being the minister of the gospel He has called me to be. I can be faithful to pray. I can be faithful to the people He has put into my life.

Guess what? If I don't do it, somebody's going to do it. If you don't sing the way God has called you to sing, there are a hundred thousand other people who God can raise up in your place. They can do what God has called you to do. A hundred thousand other Judy Jacobses could be raised up overnight. But if I'm faithful to Him, if I respond with active faith to what He says to me, I can walk in the strength and the joy of His Spirit while I fulfill His call on my life.

God doesn't hide His promises from us. They ring loudly for us to hear. God Himself does not want you to miss your moment. He will direct your feet onto the right paths. He will work everything out for the good, as long as you keep looking to Him:

> We know that all things work together for good to those who love God, to those who are the called according to His purpose. For whom He foreknew, He also predestined to be conformed to the image of His Son, that He might be the firstborn among many brethren. Moreover whom He predestined, these He also called; whom He called, these He also justified; and whom He justified, these He also glorified.
>
> What then shall we say to these things? If God is for us, who can be against us? He who did not spare His own Son, but delivered Him up for us all, how shall He not with Him also freely give us all things? Who shall bring a charge against God's elect? It is God who justifies. Who is he who condemns? It is Christ who died, and furthermore is also risen, who is even at the right hand of God, who also makes intercession for us. Who shall separate us from the love of Christ? Shall tribulation, or distress, or persecution, or famine, or nakedness, or peril, or sword? As it is written: "For Your sake we are killed all day long; we are accounted as sheep for the slaughter."
>
> Yet in all these things we are more than conquerors through Him who loved us. For I am persuaded that neither

death nor life, nor angels nor principalities nor powers, nor things present nor things to come, nor height nor depth, nor any other created thing, shall be able to separate us from the love of God which is in Christ Jesus our Lord.

—Romans 8:28–39

NOTES

CHAPTER 1
WHAT *IS* YOUR MOMENT?

1. Rod Parsley, *Daily Breakthrough* (Lake Mary, FL: Charisma House, 1998), March 6.

2. Jim Earl Swilley, *A Year in the Now* (Conyers, GA: Church in the Now Publishing, 2002), June 9.

3. Oswald Chambers, *My Utmost for His Highest*, ed. James Reimann (Grand Rapids, MI: Discovery House, 1992), June 6.

CHAPTER 2
PURSUING YOUR MOMENT

1. Parsley, *Daily Breakthrough*, February 11.

2. From "Ordination," a tract reprinted from *Good News* magazine, North Melbourne, Australia, in the 1920s. As quoted in Wayne E. Warner, *Only Believe!* (Ann Arbor, MI: Servant, 1996), 167.

3. Rick Renner, *Sparkling Gems From the Greek* (Tulsa, OK: Teach All Nations, 2003), 102.

4. Ibid., 147.

CHAPTER 3
EXPECTING THE UNEXPECTED

1. Chambers, *My Utmost for His Highest*, June 11, emphasis added.

Chapter 4
Praise Wins the Battle

1. From the weekly e-mail message of Francis Frangipane for July 27, 2007, adapted from a chapter in the book *The Three Battlegrounds*. Francis Frangipane Ministries, http://frangipane .org/.

Chapter 5
Do You Think You're Disqualified?

1. Mike Murdock, *The Wisdom Key Devotional* (Fort Worth, TX: The Wisdom Center, 2005), 24.

2. Renner, *Sparkling Gems From the Greek*, 425.

3. Ibid., 429–430.

4. Ibid., 433.

5. Chambers, *My Utmost for His Highest*, June 19.

Chapter 6
Imparting the Anointing

1. Paul M. Gouled, *The Power of Impartation* (Las Vegas: The International Church of Las Vegas, 1982).

2. Ibid.

3. Dr. Shirley Arnold, Pastor of Tree of Life Church of Lakeland, FL, personal communication.

4. Parsley, *Daily Breakthrough*, August 12.

5. Murdock, *The Wisdom Key Devotional*, 24.

6. Chambers, *My Utmost for His Highest*, June 10.

CHAPTER 7
GOD'S STRONG ANOINTED

1. Francis Frangipane, *This Day We Fight: Breaking the Bondage of a Passive Spirit* (Grand Rapids, MI: Chosen Books, 2005), 95–96.

CHAPTER 8
MADE TO MENTOR

1. Murdock, *The Wisdom Key Devotional*, 25.

2. Renner, *Sparkling Gems From the Greek*, June 16.

3. Parsley, *Daily Breakthrough*, March 1.

CHAPTER 9
THE GUMPTION TO GO!

1. Facts about Abraham Lincoln adapted from The History Place, "Lincoln Timeline," http://www.historyplace.com/lincoln/index.html (accessed January 28, 2008).

2. Swilley, *A Year in the Now*, June 13.

Stand Strong
through all of *Life's Moments*

If you have been encouraged and challenged by Judy Jacobs in *Don't Miss Your Moment*, here is another book, written in the same straightforward, gutsy, encouraging style, that we think you will enjoy:

STAND STRONG

HOW TO BECOME CONFIDENT IN YOUR CALLING, ACHIEVE STRENGTH THROUGH YOUR TRIALS, AND PREVAIL AGAINST ALL ODDS

JUDY JACOBS
AUTHOR OF *TAKE IT BY FORCE!*

978-1-59979-066-4 / $14.99

What do you do when you can't go on?

When you've tried everything but nothing works? You just **STAND**! Best-selling author Judy Jacobs shares strategies that will change the way you approach troubles in your life.

Visit your local bookstore.